THE SPARK OF LEARNING

TEACHING AND LEARNING IN HIGHER EDUCATION

James M. Lang, Series Editor

THE
SPARK
OF LEARNING

Energizing the College
Classroom with the Science
of Emotion

SARAH ROSE
CAVANAGH

WEST VIRGINIA UNIVERSITY PRESS

MORGANTOWN · 2016

24 23 22 21 20 19 18 17 16   1 2 3 4 5 6 7 8 9

ISBN:

cloth: 978–1-943665–32–7
paper: 978–1-943665–33–4
epub: 978–1-943665–34–1
pdf: 978–1-943665–35–8

Library of Congress Cataloging-in-Publication Data is available from
the Library of Congress

Cover design by Than Saffel

For Noelle,
my contagious fire

When . . . talking with student-teachers about what makes a good teacher, or reminiscing about teachers in one's own schooling experiences, encountering the term "enthusiasm" is almost inevitable. The term usually is applied to those teachers who had a certain, contagious fire in them, who burned for their subject and transmitted interest, curiosity and joy for learning and subject related tasks.

—Melanie M. Keller and colleagues, "Feeling and Showing"

Emotions are at the heart of what it means to be human.

—Elaine Fox, *Emotion Science*

CONTENTS

ACKNOWLEDGMENTS

First of all, I'd like to thank the series editor and my good friend Jim Lang for seeing the potential of a book in me with very little evidence to go on, for his assured guidance at every step in the process of its completion, and for many laughs along the way. Thanks also to Mike Land, our writer's group companion, who offered much encouragement, many great edits, and always uplifting dog stories. I owe some appreciation to our writing haunt, the Nu Café in Worcester, Massachusetts, and the Smart-Water it offers. (It seemed to help.) Thank you as well to Michele Lemons and Phil Opitz, who provided helpful feedback on some of the scientific background sections of the book.

My family has always been a deep source of writing inspiration for me—especially my grandmother and poet Margery Smith Cavanagh, my aunt and novelist/pianist/puppeteer/photographer Eliza Praetorius, and my father and poet William Cavanagh. Thank you for all of the encouragement and close readings over my lifetime; hopefully this book is lacking in the "melodrama and multiple climaxes" that plagued my adolescent fiction. On the teaching side, sincere gratitude is due to my mother Rosemary Cavanagh. When you've been helping grade papers since elementary school, it is sort of inevitable that you eventually find yourself at the front of a classroom. And to Jennifer (Sm) DiCorcia, coinstructor and partner in crime, for making the first few years of college teaching so much fun I couldn't imagine not doing it for the rest of my life.

I wouldn't be in the position to write a book such as this without the people who opened the doors to my current career. So a heartfelt thank you to Lisa Shin for making a career in academia a possibility, to Heather Urry for offering me a post-doctoral spot on her scientific dream team, and to Assumption College for becoming my academic home.

Finally, deep thanks to my partner Brian Chandley for supporting my every move since we were kids, lying in the grass dreaming of dogs and fireplaces and *reaching for the stars from the confines of our cells*. You make it all possible.

PREFACE

In graduate school, professor Holly Taylor of Tufts University gave me and my fellow classmates this advice on how to present an audience with new information (channeling Aristotle, if Google can be trusted): "Tell them what you're going to tell them, then tell them, then tell them what you've told them."

I found this so convincing that I am going to tell you what I'm going to tell you *twice*.

Here is the short version: I am going to argue that if you want to grab the attention of your students, mobilize their efforts, prolong their persistence, permanently change how they see the world, and maximize the chances that they will retain the material you're teaching them over the long term, then there is no better approach than to target their emotions. I will advise that you consider the emotions of your students when managing how you present yourself to the class, when designing your syllabus and assignments, when considering which activities to include in a given class session and how to frame those activities, and when grading and providing feedback to your students.

As a teaser of sorts, below are some of the proposed techniques you will find scattered throughout the chapters to come. I will suggest that you:

- intentionally confuse your students
- kick back and watch some popular movie trailers together
- engage in a little role-playing
- teach your students how to breathe

- tell stories about your own failures as a student
- flip how you grade
- let go of guilt and instead put sleep, exercise, and leisure at the forefront of your priorities
- spend some good time on YouTube watching silly videos with your students
- completely change how you ask questions of your students
- decide once and for all to ban technology in the classroom—or else, allow liberal use of it

Some of these suggestions have been tested in applied, rigorously controlled experimental designs, and others are supported by more basic research being conducted in laboratories and classrooms on emotion science, neuroscience, and education around the world. I'll share this evidence with you as we go, and each chapter will also have a list of suggestions for further reading if you find your appetite whetted.

So without further ado, let me . . . um, tell you what I'm going to tell you some more.

INTRODUCTION

Once More, with Feeling

I sat in my first college class with pen nervously poised, ready to absorb every word my professor had to say. I imagined that he would stand at the front of the class and stiffly, yet drolly—and preferably with an English accent—impart the wisdom of his many years in the field of psychology. Instead, the late, great Michael Fleming of Boston University stalked into the room with all the zeal of a velociraptor. He spent the semester alternately delighting and terrorizing us, telling shocking tales straight from the therapist's couch; hissing *Mystery Science Theater 3000*-style psychological commentary on scenes from popular movies; and gleefully creeping up on sleeping students to startle them awake. It was my favorite class of a very long educational career, and it was a rollercoaster of emotions.

The lay assumption seems to be that learning is a dry, staid affair best conducted in quiet tones and ruled by an unemotional consideration of the facts, and historically we have constructed our classrooms with this in mind. In this book I will make the argument that if we want to truly motivate and educate our students, we are much better off targeting their emotions. In making this argument I will bring to bear evidence from the study of education, psychology, cognitive science, and neuroscience, as well as share concrete examples of successful activities from a variety of disciplines in higher education. My area of expertise, and the source of many of the arguments I will make in this book, is called affective science. *Affect* is a word that encompasses not only emotional states but also many other experiences that involve pleasure, displeasure, and physiological arousal (e.g., motivation, physical pain) and which doesn't assume that our various emotions are discrete and separate entities (less the Pixar film *Inside Out*, and more of a continuum).

Mary Helen Immordino-Yang, educational psychologist and recipient of the Award for Transforming Education through Neuroscience, asks us to consider a hypothetical student hard at work on a physics problem. Let's call her Beth. One might expect physics, as one of the "hard" sciences, to be relatively unemotional. However, Immordino-Yang (2011) steps us through Beth's journey as she solves this problem, detailing the role of emotions at each step. First, why is Beth solving this problem at all? She could be motivated by some combination of anticipating rewards (good grades, her teacher's approval), fear of her parents' censure if she doesn't do well in the class, innate curiosity about the problem, and/or the desire for future career success. All of these sources of motivation are affective in nature. Beth may also face the challenge of regulating worry that her skills aren't a match for the problem at hand. A rich literature on the phenomenon of stereotype threat—namely, that people concerned about fulfilling a known stereotype about their group actually perform worse—suggests that Beth may be particularly struggling with these anxieties because she is a woman and she is aware of the stereotype that women don't perform well in math and science (Spencer, Steele, and Quinn, 1999).[1] Finally, she may work her way through the problem by breaking it into pieces and trying different strategies, chasing down those strategies that result in a feeling of reward and avoiding those strategies that lead to feelings of frustration.

Reflecting on Beth's experience, you might be surprised at how integrally emotion is woven into the experience of learning.

This surprise is rooted in a long history of viewing emotion and cognition (the latter being the processes involved in thinking, perceiving, and reason) as not only separate but somehow at odds with one other. Increasingly, neuroscience research indicates that the brain systems involved in emotion and those involved in cognition are not, as traditional accounts would have had us believe, separate systems pulling us in opposite directions. Rather, as we'll see in subsequent chapters, overlapping circuits are responsible for both, and the biochemical bases for each are very similar. As we'll also see, this is no coincidence. Emotions were evolutionarily selected for because they influence motivation—driving us toward things that benefit our survival and reproduction (high-calorie foods, attractive sex partners) and away from things that threaten our health or well-being (venomous spiders, rotten food). But they also influence learning—tagging certain experiences and skills as important and thus critical to both attend to and remember. From this perspective, it is perhaps unsurprising that the neural mechanisms underlying emotion, motivation, and learning are so intertwined.

Emotions and Decision-Making

Nearly every moment in your life presents you with a decision. Should you stay, or should you go? Do you respond to your friend's story with a silent sympathetic touch on her arm, or do you confront the illogical nature of her thinking? Do you continue working on your book chapter, or do you flip over to Facebook? We like to think that we make these sorts of decisions using reason, considering our long-term goals, what is best for our friend, and our progress on work, respectively. However, a wealth of psychological research suggests that this calculating, logical approach is not really how we decide. Rather, our decision-making is both fueled and guided by emotions.

One of the most influential thinkers on the role of emotion in decision-making is Antonio Damasio. He and his wife Hanna Damasio famously studied the decision-making ability of people with damage to a portion of the brain's frontal lobes called the ventromedial prefrontal cortex. They discovered that people with damage to this area of the brain as the result of stroke or trauma suddenly had tremendous difficulty making decisions. Critically, these patients seemed to have the greatest trouble prioritizing options in their decision-making. In Damasio's popular book *Descartes' Error: Emotion, Reason, and the Human Brain* (2005) he describes a case study of a man he calls Elliot—a successful businessman and father who was diagnosed and treated for a brain tumor located in the ventromedial prefrontal region. Following his surgery, Elliot's health recovered remarkably and his performance on a variety of spatial, memory, and attentional tasks was unimpaired. But his family reported that he was having a lot of difficulty with daily life, mostly surrounding social decision-making—decisions like which among a number of tasks was the most important to complete, where to go to dinner, and how to behave at a dinner party.

Damasio noticed three things: first, along with impairments in social decision-making, Elliot's emotional reactions also seemed blunted; second, his difficulty with decision-making seemed to center around an inability to judge which of a number of options might be the best; and third, he had both of these things in common with many other patients with ventromedial prefrontal damage. These clues led Damasio to propose his seminal theory of decision-making—that a person without a damaged brain tends to weigh options by running through the possible ramifications of that decision and how he or she would feel after each option, checking in with bodily reactions and feelings to each, and then choosing the one that feels the best. This process occurs quickly and indeed often unconsciously, but Damasio argues that we do this constantly—when deciding what clothes to wear in the morning, whether to risk parking illegally or to walk through the downpour from the legal parking spot, whether to change careers. In the words of Immordino-Yang and Damasio, "most, if not all, human decisions, behaviors, thoughts, and creations, no matter how far removed from survival in the homeostatic sense, bear the shadow of their emotive start" (2007, p. 7). Lacking an ability to check in with emotions, Damasio's patients were lost in a sea of options and lacking a compass.

As is often the trajectory in psychology, these few illustrative case studies were followed by much larger and more rigorous studies probing exactly which abilities are governed by the ventromedial prefrontal cortex and how emotions (in particular, reward processing) are implicated in decision-making (Bechara, Damasio, and Damasio, 2000; Naqvi, Shiv, and Bechara, 2006). While the simple account of emotion's influence on decision-making has become more complex with the addition of a number of qualifiers (Volz and Hertwig, 2016), this compelling body of work nonetheless indicates that emotions are likely guiding your hand in every decision you make—from which three plums to select from a basket of fruit to whether to leave your spouse—and, in many cases, relying on your feelings is more effective than attempting to logic things out by focusing on the details (Mikels, Maglio, Reed, and Kaplowitz, 2011; though not always Volz and Hertwig, 2016). It is not hard, then, to suppose that emotions are similarly guiding our students in every stage of their learning, from selecting which courses to take in a given semester to deciding how willing they are to participate in the discussion you're trying to drum up the Tuesday before Thanksgiving.

Indeed, in a demonstration of how emotions play out during the process of learning, Sidney D'Mello and Art Graesser (2012) asked students to track their emotions while they were being tutored by a computer program. Their analyses revealed that the students experienced frequent oscillations among states of confusion, frustration, and engagement/positive emotions, suggesting that the students were motivated to resolve the states of confusion and boredom, that they were rewarded by positive emotions such as delight, and that they sequenced through cycles of these emotions as they learned. Thus, emotions are not only guiding decisions but also motivating the process of learning itself.

In a powerful study that previews many of the points I will be making throughout this book, Alex Buff, Kurt Reusser, Katrin Rakoczy, and Christine Pauli (2011) examined both the precursors and the results of positive emotions in the classroom. Their participants were 682 eighth and ninth graders learning about the Pythagorean theorem over the course of their school year. They assessed students via pretests at the start of the school year, postinstruction tests after lessons, and follow-up tests several weeks after the lessons to gauge the students' understanding of the material and their ability to apply it. The researchers measured beliefs about competence ("I have a talent for mathematics"), levels of positive activating emotions during the lesson (excitement, stimulation, appeal, and interest), cognitive activity ("I was able to follow the teacher's explanations"), and motivation (in the forms of perceived challenge and expectations of success). Their results revealed that students who reported experiencing a greater number of positive emotions like excitement and interest during the lessons were also more cognitively activated—they engaged with the material more extensively. While positive experiences didn't relate directly to higher posttest scores, they did relate indirectly through cognitive activation. That is, more interest and curiosity led to greater engagement with the material, and it was this engagement with the material that led to better learning performance.

This finding, in essence, sums up the thesis of this book. As teachers, our end goal is to maximize student learning. We typically try to accomplish this by coaxing our students into performing better, paying more attention, dedicating more intellectual resources to class material, and procrastinating less; the traditional form this coaxing takes is a dangling of grades over their heads. In this book I will argue that a more effective route than focusing on evaluating students (though, of course, that will always play a role in the classroom) is employing tactics suggested by affective science. The classroom setting is already a highly charged emotional atmosphere; why not harness that power and direct it at learning?

What This Book Is Not

I opened with an anecdote about my favorite professor, Michael Fleming, and here I'd like to round out this introduction with some words of wisdom from him. In his class on personality psychology, we began the semester with an overview of the rise and the decline of the teachings of Sigmund Freud and those who followed in his tradition, the field of thought known as psychoanalysis. After this brief review of the stark shift away from psychoanalytic thought in much of contemporary psychology, he bellowed a "But!" Our whole class jumped in our seats and riveted our attention to him. He continued, softly but intensely: "We. Will. Know. What. We. Are. Not." And then we went on to spend the entire semester learning about psychoanalytic theory.

In this vein, I would like to take a moment early in the book to clarify some things that this book is *not* so as to address up front some skeptical questions that may have arisen as you read this introduction. First, I am not going to argue that we should slavishly tailor every moment of our students' education so that their education is a four-year trip to an amusement park. A great deal of learning involves working with the unknown, failing at tasks, sloughing through inherently uninteresting problems, butting one's head against text that seems incomprehensible, and so on. These experiences are not only unavoidable but probably also essential to learning, and no amount of trickery could wave them away for our students. Moreover, as we'll review, one of the most effective ways of engendering interest and motivation is to challenge students, to push them to the outer limits of their skills—and sometimes a bit beyond. We're not going to coddle our students; we've going to energize them to work harder than ever before.

Second, when we begin to consider intentionally crafting the impression we make on students in order to maximize their motivation and learning, I will not be proposing a one-size-fits-all solution. I'm not advocating that every lecturer should be relentlessly upbeat and shower students with excessive praise. That probably works well for some people, but as we can see with my favorite professor, sometimes being unpredictable, dramatic, and sharply critical can also work. Other lecturers stride across the stage in full business suits with a steely intimidating gaze and students eagerly perk up and scribble down every note. Still others may sit quietly and draw students in by beautifully reading prose or speaking passionately and eloquently about ideas. Being vibrant often means being vibrantly yourself. Thus, I'm not going to advise that you act any certain way, but will instead provide a series of tips aimed at letting your true self shine, and recommend that you be mindful of conveying that self accurately and inspirationally to your students.

Third (and this is a hard pill for me to swallow), not all of the advice in this book is empirically validated—that is, supported by rigorous experimental research. Wherever such evidence is available I include it, and I searched far and wide for the latest, best scientific research on each topic. But many of these ideas are still being formulated and tested, and so some of the suggestions are simply reasonable ideas from various sources, including my own experience and that of other people in higher education I interviewed. I look forward to seeing them put to the test in controlled experiments in the years to come.

Finally, it may irritate you that we need to think this hard about motivating our students. *That should come from within,* you might think. *When I was a student I was engaged by the ideas, by the work, and by my desire for a future career, not by a professor's flashy performance or activities designed to trick me into paying attention.* I'm sure that a subset of our students *are* deeply intrinsically motivated and would succeed no matter who was standing at the front of the room and which activities they were asked to complete. But many of our students have a raft of other concerns besides their intellectual growth—from their personal struggles with mental health, to caring for their families at home, to navigating their social worlds. They may be paying their hard-earned tuition dollars primarily to earn a job-focused degree and then carry on with the rest of their lives and have not a care in the world for the broader scholar we are trying to make of them. Intelligent people might disagree whether or not this is students' prerogative. But regardless of your perspective on the growing "businessification" of higher education, if you implement some of the strategies we are going to consider together, even your reluctant students may find themselves more engaged than they ever expected they could be. You may go far further in shaping their minds and hearts than if you simply presented them with the work and expected *them* to bring the enthusiasm and interest to the table.

What This Book Is

In working together to understand what this book is not, I may have fulfilled the teachings of one former instructor while betraying the teachings of another. Richard Paul was my high school social studies teacher, and he developed and taught us his own program for writing academic papers; it was called analytical thinking, and it focused on identifying clear, direct operational definitions for any terms or arguments we were making, what he called "defining attributes" of an event, work, or thesis. He would lose his temper whenever anyone tried to define something by telling him what it was not. "If you see a lion about to chomp down on your best friend," he'd implore, "are you going to shout, 'You are *not* about to be struck by lightning?!' "

To satisfy this new ghost of Sarah's educational past, let us now consider what this book *is*. First and foremost, this book is going to make the argument that, as writer and self-improvement guru Dale Carnegie once argued, "When dealing with people, remember you are not dealing with creatures of logic, but creatures of emotion." We are going to examine the psychological and neuroscientific evidence, from studies of people with damaged frontal lobes to assessments of student experiences during instruction, that suggests that Carnegie was not wrong.[2]

In part I, I will endeavor to convince you of the merit of this book's central thesis—which is that you can be a more effective teacher, leading your students to greater heights of learning—if you know some basic tenets of affective science and apply them in your classroom. I will do this first by answering the question, why emotions? In chapter 1 we will consider the science and neuroscience of emotions—what they are, what they're for, and what effects they have on our nervous system and behavior. This chapter will lay the scientific groundwork for the chapters to come. In chapter 2 we'll consider the marriage of emotions and education. What do emotions do for us, and for our students? Specifically, I'll marshal evidence that emotions grab attention, hijack working memory, enhance long-term memory for information, and engender motivation.

Thus convinced of the merits of applying affective science in the classroom, we'll move on to part II, a series of chapters with specific advice to be implemented in the classroom. Chapter 3 will consider you, the instructor, and the best ways of conveying to your students your genuine interest and enthusiasm for both your subject matter and their intellectual progress. Chapter 4 will tackle a series of what I'll call knowledge emotions—namely, interest, curiosity, and flow—and we'll contemplate how to build activities and assignments that maximize these affective states. In chapter 5 we'll evaluate some of the longer-term challenges to student performance, in the form of self-regulation: how do we encourage our students to prolong their persistence, to go the extra mile in their work? Finally, in chapter 6 we'll spend some time discussing what happens when things go emotionally wrong in the classroom. We'll review literature on emotional bumps in the road like classroom incivilities, procrastination, and social loafing on group assignments.

If I have done my job right, then you should finish the book not only with an array of specific tools from affective science to test out in your classroom but also convinced of George Orwell's assertion that "the energy that actually shapes the world springs from emotions."

NOTES

1. There have been some failures to replicate these effects (e.g., Flore and Wicherts, 2015).
2. As we'll see, however, Carnegie was not exactly right. Current neuroscientific theory would suggest that rather than this being a dichotomy, it is more that we are creatures of both logic and emotion, and that logic itself is emotional.

Part I

Foundations of Affective Science

1

THE SCIENCE (AND NEUROSCIENCE) OF YOUR EMOTIONS

At some point tonight you are likely to wrap up your day's cares, put on some form of loose-fitting clothing, and lay yourself down on a horizontal surface in order to vividly hallucinate for several hours. Most of these dreams will fade from your consciousness without ever making it into your memory stores, and you'll wake into the bright light of morning and carry on with your life unaffected. More rarely, you will instead awaken abruptly in the dark, terrified: heart pounding, dry-mouthed, and gasping. You wake because one of your dreams effectively convinces you that your very survival is at risk. Nightmares are fictions created by our sleeping brains that evoke an intense emotional response, and when you have one you experience the all-encompassing effects a state of terror can have on your body, mind, and motivation.

What Are Emotions?

Emotions such as fear are complex, multifaceted phenomena that combine experiential elements ("feelings"), physiological reactions (palms sweating, heart racing, brain activation patterns changing), and social and expressive components (facial expressions, body language). This is commonly called the trifecta of emotion—feelings, physiology, and expression. Many philosophers (e.g., Nussbaum, 2003) and psychologists (e.g., Gross,

2015) also point to the critical role of values in emotional experience. We experience something as emotional because something has changed in our internal or external milieu that either *promises* something of value (praise, social engagement, goal attainment, or good fortune, all leading to varieties of pleasure) or *threatens* something we value (goal frustration leading to anger, loss leading to grief, physical jeopardy leading to fear). We might thus do well to add appraisals of value to our trifecta of emotion.

What purpose do emotions serve? Most emotion researchers point to their critical role in our evolutionary success. Imagine you are on a picnic in the woods, and a rather large, scaly green snake slithers over your foot. If you lacked the capacity to experience emotions, you might stop and assess the situation in a painfully slow and laborious manner: *What is this object? Is it friend or foe? Is it poisonous?* By the time you finish this slow reasoning process, you might be twitching in the throes of death from the snake's venomous bite.

Most of us do not have this trouble. The moment we feel the distinctive dry slither we spring up, flailing our limbs about (behavior), our faces contort and we shout our alarm (expression), and our heart races, pumping blood to our muscles in preparation for flight (physiology). Somewhere in there—there is a lot of disagreement about at what stage and by which processes this occurs—we become aware that we are afraid (feelings). Our fast—and largely unconscious—emotional response has just saved us from a potentially life-threatening situation.

Many emotion researchers believe evolutionary pressures for survival and reproduction are the reason our basic emotional systems developed. We can create similar scenarios to that of the encounter with the snake for many of the most basic or prototypical emotions (anger, sadness, fear, surprise, disgust, and joy), whereby the emotion either moves us farther from life-threatening dangers like our snake or toward rewarding situations that might hold life-sustaining (the high-calorie Danish pastry you just ordered at Starbucks) or reproductive (the pretty woman in line next to you who just shot you a telltale eye flash) value.

People who study emotion belong to the field of research called affective science. Some of the most vigorous debates in this field surround the extent to which these emotions can be thought of as discrete entities. Some scientists align themselves with a view of emotions as distinct prepackaged programs, like apps on one's computer ("A snake! Double-click on FEAR!"). Others argue that emotional experiences are instead complex, interrelated systems of body, brain, and mind that generally predispose us to approach rewarding and avoid punishing situations but that are exquisitely sensitive to modulators such as situational context and relevant past experiences. Many others see the value of both of these perspectives, depending on the emotion, the situation, and which aspect of the trifecta they are studying.

Beyond what an emotion actually is, philosophers, psychologists, and neuroscientists also disagree on the extent to which emotions can or can't be differentiated from emotion-like phenomena such as moods, appetites, and drives. Let's consider moods first. Many scientists distinguish between emotions and moods by defining emotions as momentary, short-lived phenomena that have a direct object and a direct goal, whereas they define moods as longer lasting, sometimes on the order of hours or even days. Defined as such, moods also aren't as tied to specific internal or external stimuli. If you're in the grip of anger (an emotion), you likely know exactly what it is that you are angry about: it is in the forefront of your mind, central to what you are currently thinking about. Your anger is also likely transient, rising and dissipating rather quickly. But if you're grumpy (that is, in a mood), you might not know exactly why. You can hazard some guesses—perhaps a combination of your overdue tax return, a low level of caffeine, and the fact that a love interest hasn't responded to your text—but the precise causes are often unknown. A mood can also fade in and out of your awareness as you move from task to task, sometimes fading back, sometimes coming to the forefront.

These general distinctions between emotions and moods notwithstanding, there are many examples that blur the lines between them. For instance, a big fight with your significant other or rumors of imminent layoffs can affect your feelings for days. The time scale and strength of your feelings might match the definition of a mood, but the clear tie to an environmental stimulus matches the definition of an emotion. The dividing line between emotions and moods is thus not always such a bright one.

Drives and other motivational states also have much in common with emotion: they involve goals, invoke approach or avoidance behavior, impact neurochemistry and hormonal responses, and have evolutionary significance. In her book *Upheavals of Thought: The Intelligence of Emotions* (2003), philosopher Martha Nussbaum describes the following as characteristics of emotions proper, but we could also easily map these characteristics onto drives such as the sex drive:

> their urgency and their heat; their overwhelming force; their connection with important attachments, in terms of which a person defines her life; the person's sense of passivity before them; their apparently adversarial relation to "rationality" in the sense of cool calculation or cost-benefit analysis. (p. 22)

To further understand what is and is not an emotion, we can turn to the work of Lisa Feldman Barrett, a psychologist and director of the Interdisciplinary Affective Science Laboratory at

Northeastern University. Barrett has made a career of upending traditional theories of emotion; she is a passionate adherent to the camp that argues that the various emotions we feel are *not* like apps on our smartphones. She disagrees that specific emotions have readily identifiable and distinct underlying patterns of brain activation, bodily reactions, and behavior. Rather, she argues that emotions arise when we feel changes in our body, then look to a situation to explain why we might be feeling a certain way, and use past experiences and cultural ideas to label the present experience in terms of specific, discrete emotions. Barrett criticizes the tendency of early neuroscientific studies of emotion to ascribe specific patterns of brain activation (those brightly colored "blobs" you sometimes see splashed on images of the brain in the media) to specific emotion, labeling this blob the "anger area" or that blob the "happiness area." She notes,

> If emotion blob-ology is wrong, how does your brain make emotions? It constructs instances of happiness, sadness and the rest via several general-purpose systems that work together. These systems span your entire brain. One system relates to your general feeling of your body. Another represents your knowledge from your past experiences. These and other systems—which are not exclusive to emotion—converge to make an instance of emotion when you need one. So happiness and fear are not brain blobs— they are whole-brain constructions. (Barrett and Barrett, 2015)

While Barrett has focused more on understanding how distinct emotions (anger, fear, or guilt) may or may not differ strongly from one another in how they're constructed, we can easily extend her model to understanding how emotions, moods, drives, and other affective states may or may not differ strongly from one another in how *they're* constructed. If the various emotions are the result of underlying systems of body and brain that can be assembled in different combinations and amounts, like ingredients in a recipe, so too we could imagine emotions and moods sharing underlying systems (ingredients) but differing in intensity, time scale, and/or degree of relationship to external events. Both deep hunger and boredom with the work you're doing may motivate the same behavior of approaching the cookie jar, and joy at discovering a new pregnancy and drinking a tall glass of water after a run in the hot sun may both involve activation of reward-related dopaminergic pathways in the brain. The sadness you feel when you first hear of a personal loss is probably not an entirely different category of experience from the sadness that will plague you for the days and weeks afterward.

If these lines are all so blurry, why draw them at all? To perform science, we need to clearly define the variables we're interested in studying, and this leads to a certain amount of necessary phenomena splicing. We need to carefully sort and describe experiences if we want any hope of discerning patterns and relationships among them. At times, this careful sorting can become a sort of gospel, and we forget how interrelated and messy the processes we're studying really are—which is part of Barrett's call to arms to reexamine how we think about emotion.

In this book on how affective science (broadly construed) informs the practice of teaching, we'll consider all of these affectively tinged experiences as relevant to our concerns: emotions, moods, drives, and motivational forces. For reasons of ease and readability I will sometimes refer to these phenomena under the umbrella terms *emotion* and *affect*, but please know that I acknowledge the challenges and complexities to defining these phenomena throughout.

With that all said, before we dive into how affective processes engender better learning, we first have to understand a little better how they manage to have such profound effects on our experience. To understand *that*, we first have to take a little tour through Woody Allen's "second-favorite organ."

The Brain

All of human experience occurs in the nervous system. Every sensation, every thought, every feeling relates to changes in the patterns of activation of your brain cells (like the flow of a river at a given moment), influenced by the physical machinery by which these cells communicate (like the river bed), which is itself formed in large part by the repeated activation of your brain cells (like how the river bed is formed by the flow of the water over a long period of time).[1] Thus, all of reality as you understand it is filtered first through the communication among cells of your nervous system, and what you choose to do and think from one moment to the next is in turn changing the structure and function of these same cells. This is truly a dizzying and humbling thought, and it means that essentially all learning of the type we're concerned with in the college classroom takes place by changing the circuitry of students' brains.

Your nervous system is largely made up of tiny cells called neurons that communicate with each other using chemical messengers (neurotransmitters) released into the small gap between one neuron and an adjacent neuron as a result of a brief electrical impulse within the neuron. These chemical messengers drift across the gap and bind (like a key fitting a lock) to specialized receptors on the membrane of the subsequent neurons; they either encourage or discourage that neuron from firing its own electrical potential and releasing its own chemical messengers.

Let's take a really simple example: a dog's nose brushes your palm lightly. How is this experience encoded by the nervous system? First, touch receptors on the skin of your palm are stimulated, carrying the message of the stimulation from your skin to neurons dedicated to sensation. This electrical activation is then transmitted along sensory pathways through to your spinal cord and up to your brain. From there, the activation spreads to a strip of dedicated tissue in the outermost bark-like part of your brain, the cerebral cortex, and this allows for the conscious perception of the touch, for it to be "felt."

Sights, sounds, and smells work similarly. Our representation of the world is the result of sensory energy (wavelengths of light, sound waves, mechanical energy, etc.) impinging on our sense organs (eyes, ears, and skin), and this activation spreading to the correct area of the cerebral cortex, at which point the sensation is consciously perceived (for instance, a soft damp touch on your palm). But even this simple event requires much more processing. What is the context in which this touch is happening? Were you expecting it, or startled by it? Is this your own dog, or a strange dog? How do you feel about dogs in general? Does the touch evoke pleasure, or fear? How do you react? Do you flip your hand to scratch the dog's ear and contract the muscles in your face to form a smile? Do you instead pull your hand back suddenly and contort your face into a fearful expression? Each of these possible variations of experience and resulting behavior involve contributions of different brain regions influencing various parts of this process.

Obviously, if we wanted to cover how the brain processes all of experience, we'd be here for quite a bit longer than half a chapter. We will discuss particular brain regions and their relevance to the classroom as we encounter them along the way, but let's discuss some basic principles here. One is that much of the processing of our experience is carried out by neural activity within the cortex, that thick outer cap of our brain. The cortex is made up of two hemispheres, right and left, and four functionally defined lobes. We also have many brain regions that govern various sorts of emotional and hormonal reactions deep within the brain—sometimes called subcortical structures because they lie beneath the cortex.

A lot of communication occurs among these subcortical structures, which tend to be involved in motivational and emotional processing, and the cortex, which is more involved in the conscious processing of events and also in control of behavior. When a coworker insults you during a meeting and you intentionally take a deep breath and don't retort (or punch the coworker in his or her passive-aggressive face), it is because you consciously heard the insult and processed its meaning (a cortical function, largely carried out by regions of your temporal lobes). This resulted in a warm flush of anger (due in part to the activation of certain subcortical areas, which resulted in a downstream surge of adrenaline and elevated heart rate in your body), which was then muted by your knowledge of the social norms regarding proper behavior in a conference meeting (thanks to the contribution of your frontal lobes).

The party line used to be that the subcortical structures governed emotional processing and the cortex governed cognitive processing, and each did so somewhat independently. This traditional account is breaking down as our understanding of how the brain functions continues to increase, leading Julian Kiverstein and Mark Miller to the conclusion that

> any separation of emotional and cognitive processes in the brain doesn't hold up in reality. The brain areas that neuroimaging studies identify as being active when people perform tasks that engage emotional and cognitive processes turn out to be in constant and continuous interaction. (2015, p. 10)

Or, as Nussbaum states, "Emotions are not just the fuel that powers the psychological mechanism of a reasoning creature, they are parts, highly complex and messy parts, of this creature's reasoning itself" (2003, p. 3). These quotes nicely introduce one of the central points I'll be making in this book: you can give a nice boost to cognition by tapping into emotion using your classroom techniques because emotion is already present in all of experience, perhaps even *particularly* so in cognition.

As educators we care most deeply about learning, or the long-term changes in our students' understanding of the world, their knowledge base, and their skills and abilities. After completing a class, do they have a broader, more global perspective on this shared human enterprise of ours? Do they understand how to create testable hypotheses and collect and analyze data to evaluate them? Can they now write an elegant argument or balance a budget? Looking at the breadth of changes we're interested in, we might expect that the structures and circuits of the brain involved in achieving and then retaining these very different types of skills and knowledge are extremely varied. Indeed, while we have learned a great deal about these and even more specific topics (e.g., not just how the brain "does" language but also how it learns to meaningfully parse syllables in a spoken word), the question of exactly how social experiences such as interactions in the classroom result in long-term changes in brain and behavior is unlikely to be answered any time soon.

The Promises and Limits of Applying Neuroscience to Education

In the pages that follow, we will review specific brain regions or circuits that I judge have direct relevance for the questions at hand and for which neuroscience might add to our understanding beyond studying behavior alone. Before we get there, I'd like to highlight some common concerns about bridging education and neuroscience, because there are many people in the field of education who are worried about the implications of doing so.

To begin with an example: a few years back, a study by Ming-Zher Poh, Nicholas Swenson, and Rosalind Picard (2010) received a great deal of attention in the field of education. The oft-repeated claim about the study was that while listening to lectures, students' brain activity was lulled into a state less active even than while sleeping—an alarming assertion that fit right in with the popular trend of attacking lectures as the worst practice in higher education. However, as has been pointed out by Ken Masters (2014)—and also commented on by the acerbic, popular blogger the Neuroskeptic—the figure displayed data from a single student performing a number of tasks, including attending a lecture. For starters, one cannot conclude much of anything from data gathered from only a single individual. But, most damningly, the study was *not about brain activity at all*; rather, its intent was to demonstrate the effectiveness of a new device designed to measure skin sweating at the wrist. A graph from the study that has been splashed all over the educational world, showing a flat line during lecture and spikes during other activities such as participating in lab work, doing homework, and—yes—sleeping was actually measuring degree of skin sweating, which is a better measure of how calm a person's body is than how actively engaged his or her brain is.

This is an example of what is called a neuromyth—a poorly understood and/or overapplied neuroscientific finding that could actually be harmful to educational efforts. The rise of neuromyths is one of the most frequent concerns about emphasizing the linkages between neuroscience and education. Sashank Varma, an assistant professor of educational psychology at the University of Minnesota has, along with colleagues Bruce D. McCandliss and Daniel L. Schwartz, noted some of the other most common concerns about using neuroscience to inform educational practice, including (1) the deep divide between the context of lying prone in a neuroimaging scanner and the context of being embedded in a bustling classroom full of peers; (2) the concern that localizing certain cognitive functions (for instance, reading) to specific brain regions tells us little to nothing about how best to train a person to perform this activity; and (3) the worry among educators that an inclusion of neuroscience in research on education will result in resources being channeled away from behavioral studies that hold much greater potential for real-world applications in the classroom (Varma, McCandliss, and Schwartz, 2008, pp. 141–144).

Moreover, while the last several decades have witnessed huge advances in our ability to study the human brain and the technologies we use to do so, both our understanding and our technology are still in their infancy. For example, the most commonly used measure of brain activity is functional magnetic resonance imaging, or fMRI, and it is a technique that has both impressive promise and many limitations.

To discuss one of the major limitations of fMRI, we first need to lay an old myth to rest. You have probably heard the saying that we only use 10% of our brains. This old wives' tale is so accepted by popular culture that an entire science fiction movie was constructed around its premise: in the 2014 Scarlett Johansson vehicle

Lucy, the main character accidentally ingests a drug that ramps up her brain use to 20%, 30%, and 50%; as she approaches 100%, she can stop time and levitate people. Though the film is created all in good fun, its mythical aspects start much earlier than the time at which Johansson starts changing her hair color through the power of thought. While it is certainly true that the neurons in our brains do not all fire at once—in fact, seizures are the result of uncontrolled hyperexcitation across many brain regions—we do use all the different parts of our brains at different times. Imagine you are watching the trailer for *Lucy* while undergoing an fMRI. If I were scrolling through the resulting brain scans, I would see parts of the cortex at the back of your brain light up as you processed the visual images, parts of the cortex at your temples light up as you processed the words and narrative, emotional areas under the cortex light up when something dramatic happened, and parts of the front of your brain light up as you made judgments ("This movie is terrible!") and searched your memory for related information ("When did ScarJo manage this transition between indie movie ingenue and action hero?").

In fact, engaging in almost any sort of task while awake results in such widespread brain activation that most fMRI studies have to resort to something called the subtraction method. Essentially, you devise a control task that is as similar as possible to your experimental condition except for the one thing you are most hoping to study. For instance, if you were interested in brain activation as a response to fearful faces, you would show participants pictures of twenty people with fearful facial expressions and then show the same twenty people with neutral expressions. You would then subtract out all of the brain activation that is associated with lying in the scanner, viewing pictures, thinking about the experiment, and so on, and (hopefully) end up with that brain activation that only has to do specifically with fear perception.

But this subtraction method has its own limitations. If a brain region or network is involved in both conditions, then using the subtraction method will make your data appear to indicate that a particular brain region is uninvolved, when it may actually be critical—just critically involved in both your target task and the one you happened to choose as a control. This may be particularly important for educational neuroscience, which concerns itself with broad skills that likely involve multiple regions of the brain.

If you are now feeling completely discouraged about the possible contributions of neuroscience to education, don't be.[2] John Geake, of Oxford Brookes University, along with colleague Paul Cooper (2003), make the case that scholars in both education and cognitive neuroscience need to collaborate together for the benefit of themselves and their students. They argue that educators can benefit from the current cultural cachet and political attention awarded to matters neuroscientific, and that neuroscientists can benefit from assistance in clearly identifying the practical, societal implications of their findings (which will also help with every scientist's favorite challenge: procuring grant money). In terms of benefits to students, Geake and Cooper argue that much of cognitive neuroscience can inform educational practice. As an example, they discuss studies of synaptic plasticity, or how neural communication changes at the level of the synapse as a result of experience. This work suggests that in the eternal pedagogical struggle between breadth and depth, depth should win out—that learning requires repetition that allows new pathways to develop and strengthen; thus, to maximize long-term learning and retention of material, teachers should prioritize repeated testing occasions, multiple frames of the same material, and student-led elaboration of material wherever possible. Skimming over multiple skills or topics in order to cover the most material will result in shallow learning, easily lost once the final exams are collected and students and teachers are off to celebrate their midwinter holidays.

As much as education can learn from cognitive neuroscience, so too can cognitive neuroscience learn from education. Geake and Cooper elaborate on the multiple pressing questions educators can identify for cognitive neuroscientists to investigate, setting the stage for future work: Why do some students learn more easily than others? What are the best strategies for learning new material? At what age is it appropriate to start formal schooling? As Mary Helen Immordino-Yang and Joanna A. Christodoulou note, "The more aligned neuroscientific research is with the educational research that aims to test the real-world applicability of neuroscientific findings, the more productive the contributions of each field will be to improve learning" (2014, p. 623).

To wrap up our consideration of the promises and limitations of educational neuroscience, let's circle back to Varma, McCandliss, and Schwartz's thoughts (2008) on the subject. While they relay many critiques and concerns regarding educational neuroscience, they also identify many of the opportunities at the crossroads of education and neuroscience. For instance, they point out that education has traditionally treated motivation, emotion, social factors, and learning as discrete, separate concerns in the classroom, whereas neuroscientific findings increasingly suggest that a brain circuit called the reward system, which utilizes the same neurotransmitter (dopamine), governs all four of these processes—underscoring the present book's thesis.

Chapter Summary

Psychologist and neuroscientist Elaine Fox opens her book *Emotion Science* with the bold claim that "emotions are at the heart of what it means to be human" (2008, p. xv). As we've seen, emotions certainly determine many of our motivations, decisions, and behaviors, and the circuits governing both learning and emotion overlap. In chapter 2 we'll go beyond the centrality of emotion in human experience to consider what this centrality means for our work in the classroom. As we'll see, emotions are *also* at the heart of what it means to be a scholar and a student.

Further Reading

For more on **whether emotions are discrete, separable entities** with reliable effects on behavior or instead an assembly of parts, see Barrett, Lisa Feldman, and Russell, James A. 2014. *Psychological construction of emotion*. New York: Guilford Press.

For a readable account of the **various parts of your brain that contribute to emotional experience**, see Davidson, Richard J., and Begley, Sharon. 2012. *The emotional life of your brain: How its unique patterns affect the way you think, feel, and live—And how you can change them*. New York: Penguin.

For a more thorough **overview of affective science** in general, see Fox, Elaine. 2008. *Emotion science*. New York: Palgrave Macmillan.

NOTES

1. I first encountered this analogy in a talk by neuroscientist Sebastian Seung, author of *Connectome: How the Brain's Wiring Makes Us Who We Are* (2013).
2. Every semester that I teach my neuroscience seminar, we hit a point about a third of the way in when I can sense that the entire

class thinks that all of neuroscience is essentially neurobollocks and they have lost all of their neuro-optimism. I then pull out what I call "the awe class," and we consider advances like people with quadriplegia controlling robotic limbs with the power of thought and researchers turning mouse brains transparent to study their circuitry. Despite the real limitations of neuroscience, we are living in extraordinary times.

2

THE WELLSPRING

Emotions Enhance Learning

While working on this chapter, I began swimming laps at a new outdoor pool. Surrounding the pool and neighboring buildings are some tall wooden poles, and on some of these poles there are floodlights. One of the poles has a floodlight of a strange shape and angle, and from my perspective when I slip my head out of the water for my first breath, the silhouette of the light looks for all the world like a large bird of prey. Out of all of the stimuli in my visual field, my attention hones in on this one, potentially threatening stimulus. This is a great example of emotion's ability to grab attention, and how involuntary this effect can be. It is an even better example when I tell you that this happens *every single lap*. I know that the shape is not a bird of prey about to swoop down for a tasty snack of my eyeballs. I feel impatient with myself at each lap, but I cannot unsee it; I cannot, with my supposedly powerful and sophisticated human logic and reason, shut down this basic mechanism of a potentially emotionally relevant stimulus grabbing all of my cognitive resources and directing them at the potential threat.

It is just this powerful hijacking of the brain's priorities and processing that we are going to examine for the rest of this chapter—considering how tapping into emotion will harness our students' attention, dominate their working memory resources, enhance their long-term memory consolidation, and fuel their motivation. In this chapter we'll be focusing on *how* and *why* emotions have such power over learning and performance. In the chapters in part II we'll move on to consider specific strategies for implementing emotions in the classroom.

Emotions Harness Attention

Neuroscientist Joseph LeDoux has made a career of studying how the brain processes information relevant to fear. He even has a blues band named *The Amygdaloids*, named for the amygdala, almond-shaped clusters of nuclei (we have one in each hemisphere) important for detecting biologically relevant information in our environment. LeDoux argues that our brains are so good at detecting certain survival-related stimuli (like the snake from chapter 1's picnic, or my bird of prey) that there are some neural circuits that go directly from early sensory processing areas to the amygdala, activating the body's threat response system before the information makes it all the way to the cortex to turn it into a conscious visual experience. What this means is that our bodies are getting ready to fight or flee before we have even "seen" anything in the sense that we usually mean it (i.e., the conscious experience of seeing). In a way, we can think of our attentional system from a Darwinian perspective. We have limited attention, and competition for that attention is fierce. Only the most goal-relevant items will survive this competition and win our attention. Since emotions may be processed in a privileged manner, and by definition arise because of relevance to our concerns and goals and may have implications for our survival and well-being, emotion trumps all in this battle for attention.

In the introduction we saw that emotions serve us by guiding our decision-making (as in Antonio Damasio's case study of Elliot, who suddenly lost his ability to make even the simplest decisions), and in chapter 1 we saw that they also serve us by enhancing our survival (as in the case of you leaping up and dislodging the snake from your leg without having to think about it first). But suppose we want to break down a little further the how of emotions: what are they doing at the level of the nervous system to benefit us in these ways?

One way emotions have these beneficial effects is by changing your pattern of attention. If you haven't spent a lot of time thinking about how your brain perceives the world, it may seem to you that our brains are like little video recorders, faithfully documenting everything that is happening around us at any given moment (broad attention), and storing all of this information for possible future review, should it become relevant (comprehensive memory).

In actuality, this couldn't be further from the truth. Our attention is incredibly limited—it operates a lot like a small spotlight, focusing on a narrow subset of information at any given time. In fact, our attention is so limited that if you are highly focused on one aspect of a scene, you might even miss something obvious and dramatic occurring right in front of you. The most famous experiment demonstrating this effect, called inattentional blindness, was performed by Daniel Simons of the University of Illinois at Urbana-Champaign and Christopher Chabris of Harvard University (2011), and hilariously involved a person in a gorilla costume. Simons and Chabris showed participants videos of a complicated basketball game in which people in black or white T-shirts passed two basketballs back and forth; they then asked the participants to count the number of passes made by one of the teams. This is a challenge for attention—remember that two balls are in constant motion, and you also have to note whether the color of the person's T-shirt matches the team you are tracking. Halfway through the video, a person in a large, furry gorilla costume enters the scene, stops midway, and bangs his chest dramatically. Caught up in the attentional challenge of tracking the passing balls, at least half of participants fail to see the gorilla. I don't believe I will ever tire of the looks on my students' faces in Introductory Psychology when, after showing the video, I ask, "How many of you saw the gorilla?" There are always some who see the gorilla right off, and some in the know who smirk along with me from the beginning, but the bulk of the class always looks completely bewildered until we play the video again and let them in on the joke.

Consider also that this is an example of how limited attention can be when we are fully awake, mentally engaged, and focused. We spend much of our days in states other than full waking mental engagement. We get drowsy, for one thing, and during these states not only our focused attention slips but also our very consciousness. Moreover, we are distracted by competing thoughts either passing (I can't forget to pick up milk on the way home) or quite ruminative and occupying (Is my mother going to make it out of surgery this week?). Think back to your last car trip to work; for how much of the drive were you focused on your passing surroundings, your manipulation of the car's steering wheel, your foot on the gas pedal? And for how much of the drive were you absorbed in the song that was playing on the radio that fit your mood just perfectly, the rehashing of your last encounter with that infuriating colleague, or the anticipation of your next encounter with that special someone in your life? Two things we should note about your answer: first, a good portion of your limited attention is directed inward rather than outward, further constricting the amount of information you are taking in from the world; second, what is competing for your attention is all emotional (the mood-matching song, the infuriating colleague, your beloved), and all self-relevant. This is neither a coincidence nor (entirely) contrived. One of the principal ways that emotions influence our psychological world is by grabbing our attention, shouting from the wide sea of things you could possibly pay attention to, *Me! Me!* Pay attention to *me!* Think back again to our snakes-on-a-picnic example. If emotions are going to help us survive, one of the best things they can do is to direct your limited, flawed attention to those things that may have relevance for your goals of survival and reproduction. This attention-grabbing power of emotional stimuli is one of the few human tendencies that is probably at least somewhat "hardwired," or preprogrammed, into our brains right from the start.

Therefore, when faced with a classroom of students who are potentially drowsy, stressed, and exposed to multiple sources of competing stimuli both external (the smartphones in their laps) and internal (nagging worries about whether they're going to pass the calculus exam they have next), your best route for grabbing everyone's attention and directing it to the material at hand may well be to tap into your students' emotions using your activities and assignments. This can be as straightforward as simply making the material relevant to their concerns. In this way, you are still covering the material you hoped to cover and that fit with your learning goals, but you have made it much more likely that the students' attention will be engaged. We'll discuss some more concrete tips and strategies in part II, but for now you might start percolating ways that you can introduce emotion in the classroom in order to take control of your students' spotlights and focus them on the material you want them to consider.

Emotions Maximize Working Memory Potential

Once your spotlight of attention has focused on just one subset of the complicated theatrical production that is your current situation, another psychological concept becomes critical to understanding whether your spotlight will linger there and how deeply you will process that subset of elements: that of working memory. In contrast to your long-term memory stores, your working memory is rather like a computer's RAM, or available processing capability. Your attention is a primary contributor to *what* you hold onto and mentally manipulate in working memory. Your RAM, or your working memory capacity, determines *how much* information you can hold in your current consciousness and "work" on.

You may have used an older computer where if you have too many programs open at once, they all slow and eventually stall. By keeping only one or two programs open at a time, the processing capability is spread less thinly and the programs work well. Your working memory is much the same. If you spread it too thinly, across too much information or too many types of tasks, you won't process any of the information well. This is the essence of the latest wave of antitechnology panic—all of the hoopla over "multitasking" is essentially claiming that in this era of smartphones, smartwatches, and constant texting, we're overtaxing our working memory and doing a whole lot of nothing, since we're dedicating such shallow resources to any one task or pursuit.

A famous story in my family goes like this: my mother, a junior high school teacher, was attempting to enter grades while her students worked in small groups. They were getting increasingly rowdy, as junior high students tend to do, and she kept having to speak sternly to them. Finally, she grew so angry that she abruptly shouted out loud, "Five!" Stunned silence followed . . . and they all burst into laughter. Her working memory was spread between the grading and the need to chastise the students, and one interfered with the other. Incidentally, I stopped teasing my mother about this story after a humbling moment when my then four-year-old and I were entering the house and I was juggling my bags, the mail, and her backpack and budging the dog away from the door with my leg all while she pummeled me with various requests. I finally shouted, "Noelle, I only have *one eye!*"

Cognitive load theory (CLT) considers the limited nature of students' working memory and develops a model for how working memory capacity is divided among the processes students are using (Huk and Ludwigs, 2009). It proposes that our students' limited working memory is spread among three sources of tax on working memory resources: germane (resources dedicated to the development of new learning), intrinsic (resources divided among the number of tasks and their complexity), and extraneous (resources divided to distracting or interfering thoughts or processes). CLT argues that these taxes on working memory resources are additive, and that to aid student learning we should intervene to free up as much working memory as possible for germane and intrinsic purposes, usually by reducing extraneous load.

Applying the principles of CLT to actual learning in the classroom, Thomas Huk and Stefan Ludwigs of Germany (2009) explored an innovative program designed to provide both cognitive (increasing working memory resources available for germane and intrinsic purposes) and affective/emotional support (increasing student interest, which should reduce extraneous load) for students' learning of a complicated economics problem. Intriguingly, cognitive support alone did not predict student comprehension scores. Only when cognitive support was combined with affective support did student understanding increase, leading the authors to conclude that one must consider the emotional aspects of learning when trying to intervene to increase cognitive resources. Huk and Ludwigs proposed that we modify CLT to "aCLT"—*augmented* cognitive load theory—to emphasize the importance of both cognitive and affective factors in learning.

Why was it not enough to boost working memory? Why was the emotional component so critical? While it is great to free up more working memory, there is no guaranteeing that students will use that working memory for task-related demands or learning. They are probably equally as likely to direct the free processing to distracting or extraneous processing—daydreaming, texting, and the like. It is only when you also boost their interest in the task that they then dedicate these extra resources to learning and performance.

Emotions Enhance Memory Consolidation

Where were you at 12:04 P.M. last August 12? Unless by happenstance I have chosen your birthday, it is highly unlikely that you can tell me where you were and what you were doing at that particular moment in your life, even though only mere months have passed since then. How about at 9:03 A.M. on September 11, 2001? Even though this date is well over a decade further back in your history, I'm guessing that the odds are much higher that you have a clear memory of exactly where you were and what you were doing at this moment, when the second hijacked plane struck the World Trade Center in the deadliest terrorist attack on U.S. soil. This is one example of what memory researchers refer to affectionately as a "flashbulb" memory—a memory that due to its novel and emotional circumstances feels preserved in your mind with the crispness of a photograph.

In the previous two sections, we considered how emotions harness attention and maximize working memory, so that your students are attentive and able to direct a lot of their cognitive muscle toward your class activities. However, once our classes are focused and humming, our pedagogical job is only half done. After all, we don't want our students to merely engage with the material while they are sitting in class or doing homework in their dorms; we want them to retain this information once they've shut their notebooks or laptops and moved on with their day. Indeed, we want our students to not only retain what they've learned in the short term (until the next exam) but also be forever changed by having sat through our classes. In other words, we have to consider not just how to capture the attention of our students but also how to enhance their memory.

As it turns out, the story of memory is quite similar to the story of attention. A common misunderstanding is that our brains encode all of our experiences, and that forgetting is merely an inability to access that stored information. Popular films would have us believe that if you can't remember the details of an occurrence, you can just turn to your local eccentric hypnotist, who will whip out her handy pocket watch and pull the memories out of you. But this is far from true. For one thing, only those bits of information to which you have attended can make it any further along in the process of committing them to memory. Consider the gorilla experiment we discussed earlier in this chapter. How could you possibly *remember* the gorilla if you had never noticed its existence in the first place?

But let's say that the information we'd like our students to recall is already in their spotlight of attention, perhaps because we made the material self-relevant and this focused their limited attention on the material under discussion. One of the best predictors of whether an event or information will be remembered is how emotional it is. In fact, memory's bias for emotion is among the most reliable effects we have in psychology. This shouldn't be surprising, as you may recall that one of the principal benefits of emotion is its ability to tag certain experiences and information as critical for our goals and thus worth remembering.

How are emotional memories tagged in such a way? Larry Cahill, Bruce Prins, Michael Weber, and James L. McGaugh (1994) famously demonstrated that it is in part the hormones involved in emotional response that seem to encourage the greater consolidation, or formation, of emotional versus neutral memories. In a clever and now classic experiment, they had participants listen to one of two stories while viewing accompanying images. In both of these stories, the images were the same, and there were many shared characteristics: a young boy visits the hospital and along the way is detained. But one version of the story was pretty neutral—the boy is going to the hospital to visit his father at work, and along the way sees some junk cars and a disaster drill being practiced. In another version, the story was highly emotional—the boy is struck by a car and has to be rushed to the hospital in order to have his feet reattached. When the participants returned to the lab for a memory test a week after the experiment, the people who heard the emotional version had much better memory for the details of the story than did the people who heard the neutral story. This surprised no one—again, better memory for emotional versus neutral material was a long-established finding. But the critical manipulation in the experiment was that a subset of the people hearing the emotional version of the story took a pill right before beginning the experiment. This pill blocked the hormonal component of the emotional response—specifically, it interfered with the adrenaline release and its effects. Those who swallowed the pill performed much like the people who listened to the neutral version. Their memories of the story a week later were sparse and shallow.

It turns out from later and more elaborate studies that the reason this pill was so effective was that the boost emotion gives to memory is largely the result of a cascade of neural responses. The hormones involved in the body's threat response also impact communication among brain regions like the amygdala (detecting biologically relevant stimuli) and the hippocampus (known to be important in the formation of new autobiographical memories). In Cahill's study, when you knock the hormones out of the equation with a pill, it essentially places a big roadblock in this cascade and the information is not preferentially processed by the hippocampus. It is treated like neutral information; it doesn't get the boost.[1]

But we certainly can't go around passing out pills to our students; and, in any case, we don't want to discourage memory consolidation, we want to encourage it. How best can we do that? By taking advantage of the systems nature has already built for us. By making our classroom activities emotional, we will maximize the chances that this information will receive the requisite memory boost and be retained in the longer term. For instance, in my Social, Cognitive, and Affective Neuroscience seminar we discuss how the brain maintains a body image, or a mental representation of one's own body in space. I want to drive home the idea that this body image is much more malleable than students might expect and that it delicately relies on the integration of multiple channels of input (sight, touch, vestibular sense related to balance, etc.). I also want them to remember this material. So I induce in them the startling, multisensory experience of suddenly possessing a third arm. Since a large part of one's body image has to do with the coinciding sensory information from sight and touch, you can induce a perceived third arm by combining visual information (hiding one of your real arms and providing a convincing rubber arm) and tactile information (having a volunteer stroke both the hidden arm and the pretend rubber arm at the same time, using a small paintbrush). This experience tends to be emotional (I think the scientific way to describe students' reactions to this strange experience is that they "freak out"), and thus it captures student attention and makes memory retention more likely. Finally, since I have the students working together to accomplish the illusion, it is a social experience, which as we'll see in later sections carries its own cognitive benefits. While I can't show you data to support this, I'm guessing that the third arm activity is one of the few solid memories students carry out of this course for years to come. I can only hope that along with the memory of the event itself, they also carry with them the take-home point (i.e., the malleable nature of the brain's perceptions). Otherwise I've wasted a good deal of time over the last six years explaining to colleagues why I have rubber body parts strewn around my office.

Emotions Inspire Motivation: Individual Motivation

Recently a friend of mine shared an *Onion*-style fake news article by Gabrielle Bluestone titled "Woman Discovers Her Cat Has Been Keeping a Second, Secret Human Family." The article jokes that there were many warning signs that the cat had become involved in a secret affair of the heart: "But after a few good years, Ming began coming home late, without his collar . . . he switched to a new cologne, covered up the grey in his fur and started going to the gym."

Like most good jokes, this is funny in part because it hits home. Many people can think of an experience where they observed a sudden change in the personal care habits of one half of a long-term couple, followed by a slightly less sudden change in their relationship status. While this behavior change is surely at least partly practical (i.e., the deliberate focus on improving appearance to be more attractive to a new partner), I would argue that both the cat and the philandering spouse have also experienced a sudden burst in motivation from the well of energy we tap to pursue our efforts. The emotions involved in the affair—the desire, the sense of new possibilities, and yes, even the fear of discovery and the guilt—have lit a motivational fire under our faithless friends. This energy is often focused on physical self-improvement but also often spills over into other goal-directed activity. Witness the adulterous spouse who doesn't just pick up a gym habit but pursues a promotion at work and starts playing a musical instrument.

At first blush, this argument might appear a bit strange. It may seem counterintuitive that emotions associated with an affair might benefit goal-directed activity in one's life that is completely unrelated to the relationship in question. But you might remember from our consideration of memory that when the brain detects that something in the environment is goal related and thus deserving of an emotional response, alarm centers in the brain result in the cascade of hormonal responses like the release of stress hormones and adrenaline, which yield greater consolidation of memory. These same hormones not only encourage the brain to hold on to these memories but also rev up the entire body and brain to a higher level of alertness or energy. Even if you haven't studied biology at all, you're probably familiar with adrenaline as being part of the biochemical basis for the surge of energy one gets when afraid or angry. Classroom activities and assignments designed to be emotional could yield smaller-scale primes of this system and result in students being more engaged, energetic, and enthusiastic.

You may recall our discussion of the differences between (and similarities among) emotions and moods in chapter 1. There we focused mostly on intensity, time course, and linkage with specific events or stimuli (with emotions being more intense, fast, and tied to specifics, and moods less so). Similarly, emotions and moods differ in terms of their effects on behavior. The effects of emotions are highly identifiable and immediate—you jump back in fear, you impulsively smile out of joy—but the effects of moods on behavior are less so. Guido Gendolla, director of the Geneva Motivation Laboratory at the University of Geneva, developed what he calls the mood-behavior model (MBM), which tackles how moods affect behavior, including the mobilization of effort, and posits that moods have effects on behavior because mood is used as one piece of information in the evaluation of the current task and its context. When we attempt to decide how difficult something is, whether we have the necessary skills to accomplish what is needed, how much effort it will take, and whether we have done enough, we use our current mood as one piece of information in this process. According to the model and its supportive research evidence, those in positive moods will be more optimistic about the difficulty, their skill level, and the required effort, and will persist longer than people in negative moods (Gendolla and Brinkmann, 2005). Not only that, but people in positive moods will demonstrate greater mobilization of effort (i.e., preparing to expend mental or physical resources on a task), as can be measured by activation of their cardiovascular system.

So is it the case that we should always strive to induce only positivity and positive moods in the classroom? Actually, no. Gendolla and Brinkmann demonstrate that these effects can be moderated by task difficulty: for easy tasks, people in negative moods demonstrate greater mobilization, whereas for challenging tasks, people in positive moods demonstrate greater mobilization. In addition, Klaus Fiedler and Susanne Beier of the University of Heidelberg (2014) review the literature on emotions and cognitive performance relevant to education and posit that negative moods can often lead to greater accuracy, more careful responding, and less use of often unreliable heuristics. On the other hand, positive moods *do* seem to lead to greater creativity, better self-generated inferences, and superior organization of knowledge. Flexibly responding with appropriate mood induction based on the current situation and task may be the most beneficial for students, and you should pay the most attention and effort to creating a positive climate in the classroom on days when your activities and topics require more creativity than focused attention to detail.

Thus, considering the emotional climate of your class and using activities and assignments that are emotional in nature may result in greater mobilization of effort in your students—an argument we'll visit in much greater depth in chapter 4, where we'll also examine practical ideas for ways of doing so.

Emotions Inspire Motivation: Emotional Contagion

In January 2012 some people in our country may have had a slightly tougher week, emotionally speaking, because Facebook decided it should be so. This startling revelation hit the presses and ignited a firestorm of controversy. Essentially, some researchers at Cornell University teamed up with some members of the Facebook data analytic team and decided to study the phenomenon of emotional contagion (Kramer, Guillory, and Hancock, 2014). Human beings are intensely social creatures, and we tend to first perceive and then acquire the emotions of those around us. As cheerleaders, motivational speakers, and Boy Scout troop leaders can all tell you, emotions can spread through groups and crowds quite easily. Returning to our evolutionary perspective from chapter 1, this makes a lot of sense: creatures living in social groups are probably well advised to first sense and then adopt the emotions of their larger social group. For instance, if emotions prepare us for action, and our group is tensed up and ready to fight, it may be adaptive to quickly join that preparatory stance. The main mechanism by which this occurs is likely an instinctive mirroring of expressive behavior like facial expressions and body tension, which then has corresponding effects on experience.[2]

On Facebook you can't see people's natural facial expressions, body stance, or gestures—though you can use little graphics called emoticons, and recently Facebook added a feature through which you can indicate your mood directly. But you do impart quite a lot of emotional information in the statuses you share, and these researchers decided to study whether emotions spread through social networks in a way that is similar to how they spread through crowds. To do this right they had to make sure it was a controlled test by randomly assigning people to conditions where everything about their experience was the same other than the key variable of interest.[3] Otherwise they wouldn't be able to claim that any spreading of emotion was truly due to emotional contagion.

So what did Facebook do? It selected a large number of users and randomly assigned them to either see fewer negative posts or fewer positive posts in their news feeds, and then measured the number of posts and number of emotional words the users in each group correspondingly used in the week of the manipulation. Facebook didn't delete or hide anyone's posts—you could still see everything all of your friends were doing if you went to their personal timelines—but if you were in one of the experimental groups, the posts that made it into the ticker of stories in your news feed were controlled by Facebook in an attempt to make you feel better or worse. And just as they expected, the team from Facebook and Cornell observed emotional contagion. Even in the absence of actual human face-to-face interaction, people who saw less positive content in their news feeds posted fewer positive and more negative posts than they had before being manipulated by Facebook. Correspondingly, people who saw less negative content posted fewer negative and more positive posts than they had before the manipulation. In sum, emotional contagion is such a strong effect that it may be able to spread through social networks in which users aren't even interacting in person.[4]

This study demonstrated how powerful emotional contagion can be—that it is such a strong effect that it can even spread online in superficial encounters. Multiple other studies over many years have shown that emotional contagion processes are even stronger in person, and in close-knit groups in particular (Hatfield, Carpenter, Rapson, 2014). Emotional contagion is thus likely at play in your classroom, and there are several ways in which it may manifest. The first is that your own emotions may infect your students. Several decades ago, a teacher and psychologist named Haim Ginott deduced this about his teaching, without the benefit of the intervening decades of research on emotional contagion: "I have come to a frightening conclusion. I am the decisive element in the classroom. It is my personal approach that creates the climate. It is my daily mood that makes the weather" (Ginott, 1972, pp. 15–16).

In more scientific reflections, Eva Susann Becker and her colleagues (Becker, Goetz, Morger, and Ranellucci, 2014) point out the critical role that instructor-to-students emotional contagion may play in student motivation and performance. To understand this important issue, they examined a more general form of emotional contagion they call "crossover," which considers not only the transfer of fully realized emotions but also other affectively tinged states such as burnout (on the negative side) and flow (on the positive side).

How does this affective crossover effect occur? There are multiple possibilities that could play a role, but Becker and colleagues marshal research to argue that one of the strongest contributors to crossover is a process by which instructor emotions (e.g., positive emotion) lead to changes in instructional behavior (e.g., greater enthusiasm in delivery, more extensive examples), which then leads to changes in students' feelings of value and control (which, as we'll see in chapter 5, are truly critical), and that this significantly impacts learning. This research demonstrates that teachers who reported more positive emotions are more likely to provide adequate examples, to give more clear and comprehensible explanations, to make more connections between the subject matter and the real world, and to teach with greater enthusiasm. Conversely, teachers who experience more negative emotions such as anger or anxiety are less likely to show these beneficial instructional behaviors. Thus, teachers with better emotions may use better methods, which translates into better control and value appraisals and thus better learning.

The studies providing evidence for this crossover pathway have mostly been retrospective—that is, have asked teachers and students to recall past experiences and report on them. Using this type of research limits a researcher's abilities to draw firm conclusions due to the limitations of memory and the possibility that positive experiences in the classroom get incorrectly generalized to the teacher's behaviors (or vice versa). To move research on crossover forward, Becker and colleagues decided to use a technique called experience sampling, which is just what it sounds like: a data collection technique that requires participants to report on (sample) their perceptions and reactions in real time (experience). Over two consecutive weeks, the researchers had ninth-grade students use iPods to record their emotional experiences (of enjoyment, anger, and anxiety), their perceptions of their teacher's emotions (of enjoyment, anger, and anxiety), and their perceptions of their teacher's instructional behaviors (e.g., "At the moment, my teacher explains things in a comprehensible way," or, "At the moment, I understand the aims and goals of this lesson"). Notably, the results revealed that instructional behavior and perceived teacher emotions both predicted students' feelings of anger and enjoyment, but that perceived teacher emotions directly related to student emotions regardless of instructional behavior. That is, it wasn't purely that teachers' positive emotions translated to better instruction, which translated to student emotions; rather, teacher emotions predicted student emotions above and beyond changes to instructional behavior, supporting the emotional contagion or crossover effect. It may be that the teachers' portraying positive emotions resulted in positive emotions in their students, which benefited learning for the reasons we covered in the last few sections (better attention, memory, and motivation). In chapter 3 we'll consider a variety of ways in which you can effectively take advantage of these affective crossover effects by projecting attributes like enthusiasm, confidence, and optimism.

Of course, students are also often working together, talking together, and studying together; just as your emotions are affecting your students, their emotions are affecting each other. Their levels of positive and negative emotions, their goals for their performance, and their evaluations of you, the instructor, are all linked and influencing each other. In chapter 1 we discussed how emotions serve our most basic goals, pushing us toward things good for survival and reproduction and away from things threatening or potentially infectious. Some of the most essential human goals are to develop and maintain social connections and a sense of belonging. After all, there are few things more critical to our well-being than being part of a social group—other human beings to take care of us when we're sick, gather food for us when we're lame, and take over and care for our offspring should we suddenly perish. In more modern-day terms, these other human beings give our presentation at work for us when we're out with the flu, deliver casseroles when we have a new baby or experience the sudden loss of a loved one, and pick our children up from school if we're stuck in traffic. Emotional contagion likely helps maintain smooth social cohesion. Furthermore, emotional ties with social others are powerful motivators and determinants of behavior.

In an innovative research project on the nature of collegiate experiences, Daniel F. Chambliss and Christopher G. Takacs (2014) spent over ten years studying the students on their campus at Hamilton College, interviewing them extensively and in many instances following them into their lives beyond college. They gathered information on courses taken, extracurricular participation, dormitory experiences, grades received, careers pursued, and satisfaction with the college experience. Among the many fascinating specific findings they share in their book *How College Works*, one solid theme emerged: what makes a successful college isn't the number of Nobel Prize winners at the front of classrooms or how many new science buildings are built on campus. Rather, it is the people. The best predictors of student satisfaction and success are whether students form close-knit friendships, have a mentor or two on campus with whom they develop a close relationship (it doesn't even need to be a professor), or find a meaningful social group with which to identify.

While these findings were a bit of a revelation in the world of higher education, social neuroscientists would not be surprised one bit by this central role of social experiences in determining satisfaction. One such neuroscientist is James Coan, associate professor of psychology, who has garnered quite a bit of attention in both the scientific community and in the popular press for a series of studies in which he probed the neural basis of social connection, and specifically why social connections are so beneficial when we're facing possible threat or stress (Coan, Schaefer, and Davidson, 2006). As Coan explains in his widely viewed TEDx Talk, this work grew out of an experience he had when, as a clinical psychologist, he worked with a reluctant veteran with post-traumatic stress disorder. The veteran was unwilling or unable to do some of the hard emotional work the therapy entailed, like having to relive some of his original traumas—that is, until his wife gently took his hand.

That this simple act could yield such dramatic changes in a person's ability to confront threat led Coan and his colleagues to devise a series of neuroimaging studies in which they placed people in an fMRI scanner, put them under threat, and then varied whether someone was or was not holding their hands. The researchers varied threat using a threat-of-shock paradigm. While the participants lay in the scanner, they viewed Xs or circles. When a circle appeared, they knew they were safe from shock; when an X appeared, they had a 20% chance of experiencing a slight electric shock to their ankle. During image viewing, some of the time participants did not have their hands held, some of the time their hands were held by a stranger, and some of the time their hands were held by their significant others.

Coan found that when he compared the threatening trials with and without hand-holding, the neural regions associated with threat processing were significantly less active in the hand-holding condition, and particularly less so for spouse hand-holding than stranger hand-holding. Coan has replicated this essential finding in several subsequent studies, and in some of them the social partners are not touching the participant but merely present. Together, this research suggests that when our loved ones are near, we react less to stress—and critically, we are less likely to activate structures in the brain that govern our hormonal response to stress. Excess stress hormones like cortisol have been linked to both poorer physical and emotional health and, at least in rats, in the death of neurons in stress-vulnerable (and cognition-important) areas of the brain.

But Coan was not done with us yet. In later work he decided to go one step further and investigate what happens in our brains when we observe a friend being shocked. In this study Lane Beckes, James A. Coan, and Karen Hasselmo (2013) discovered that participants' brains responded to threats to the self and threats to a close friend in a remarkably similar fashion, and that the closer the self-reported overlap in self-identity between friend and self, the stronger this correlation was. These data suggest something revolutionary about friendship—that to your brain, friendship may involve a "breach of individual separateness," and that we can see the evidence for this blurring in how the brain processes threats to both. I think we have all felt this on some level, and not just when threatened. After spending a good deal of time with a friend or romantic partner, we find ourselves mirroring their mannerisms and patterns of speech, perhaps finishing their sentences. We can carry on whole arguments with our partners that exist solely in our own heads, parrying each side effortlessly. At the end of his TEDx Talk, Coan expresses that after his first study, he began to believe that the power of hand-holding lies in the message it conveys: "I am here with you. I am you." Following his subsequent study, he now feels that the message is really, "We are here. We are here" (Coan, 2014).

How exactly might this research, mostly conducted on spouses or those in long-term friendships, shed light on our students' experiences? Bear with me through one more neuroscience study and then I'll tie it all together. This set of researchers (Lebreton, Kawa, d'Arc, Daunizeau, and Pessiglione, 2012) wanted to understand less how our emotions spread from one to another and more how our goals do. They called attention to experiences we've all had or witnessed, such as a child having no interest in a toy until another child makes a grab for it, when suddenly that toy is the *best toy ever*! One can observe similar occurrences in the realms of mate choice, job candidates, and popularity. Nothing makes something quite as enticing as knowing that *someone else wants it*. The authors use philosopher René Girard's term "mimetic desire" for this concept. In a study that is more convoluted than we need to cover, they attempted to unpack the neural underpinnings of mimetic desire, or goal contagion. In essence, participants viewed a long series of images depicting objects, some of which also depicted hands reaching out to grasp the objects. Later on, the participants rated how desirable these objects were. As expected, the authors observed a main effect of seeing someone else reach for an object—those objects that were reached for were rated as more desirable than the ones that no one seemed to want. But, notably, the strength to which this was true was predicted by brain activation in the pleasure circuit of the brain—the same circuit that is involved when you sip an alcoholic drink or laugh at a joke.

If we put together affective crossover, Coan's hand-holding experiments, and this mimetic desire study, what do we get? We get human beings who are powerfully motivated by the development of social connections, soothed by the presence of social connections in times of anxiety, and highly susceptible to the contagious effects of other people's emotions and goals. All of these are affective science principles with high potential relevance for the classroom. We've established that the classroom is a highly emotional environment, so emotional contagion is something to consider closely—maximizing the chances that your enthusiasm will infect your students (which we'll cover in chapter 3) and minimizing the chances that their emotions of frustration or lack of control will coalesce into a stubborn block of resistance (which we'll cover in chapter 6). Moreover, the classroom is also made up of a group of social beings who are often anxious and deciding how hard they want to work on some goals you are trying to impart to them. Knowing a bit about the dynamics of effort mobilization (as we'll discuss in chapter 4) and how to best create a classroom environment in which your students interpret your work together as valuable and within their control (as we'll discuss in chapter 5) may go a long way toward having an enjoyable, productive semester together.

Chapter Summary

In this chapter we've seen just how potent emotions can be in enhancing every cognitive process at play in higher education—from the initial, necessary step of attracting our students' attention, to being sure they're applying the majority of their working memory resources to class concerns, to maximizing the chances of long-term memory consolidation, to engendering motivation and enthusiasm for the course material (which, as we'll see in later chapters, will carry them through the trenches of midterm exams and a host of distracting alternatives to schoolwork).

Hopefully you are now persuaded that affective science principles can be helpful in our course preparations and in our day-to-day classroom management. This has been the *why*. Next let's consider the *how*.

Further Reading

For more details on the **science of emotions as applied to education**, see:

Immordino-Yang, Mary Helen. 2015. *Emotions, learning, and the brain: Exploring the educational implications of affective neuroscience*. New York: Norton.

Jossey-Bass (Ed.). 2014. *The Jossey-Bass reader on the brain and learning*. San Francisco: Jossey-Bass.

Sousa, David A. 2010. *Mind, brain, and education*. Bloomington, IN: Solution Tree.

NOTES

1. As with many early, classic research studies, subsequent studies have revealed that this explanation isn't the entire story. There are many other reasons why we remember emotional stimuli more than neutral stimuli (Talmi, 2013).

2. There is good evidence that expressive behavior mirroring is a principal mechanism by which emotional contagion occurs; however, a growing body of work suggests that chemosignals embedded in our sweat and inhaled through the nose may also play a role. Thus, you may find a funny or scary movie funnier or scarier than you would otherwise when in a crowded movie theater, because molecules from the secretions of people around you are taken into your body and thus influence the emotions you experience! This may or may not impact how you feel about the handfuls of popcorn you are shoveling in your mouth.

3. Usually if you are going to experiment on human beings in this way—randomly assigning them to conditions that may change their experience of life for a brief time—you have to obtain their permission first. Facebook and Cornell side-stepped this requirement by claiming that the study fell within the parameters of the data use agreement that its users acknowledge when they first sign up.

4. We should note, however, that since this study was indeed "massive," involving hundreds of thousands of participants, the researchers had the statistical power to detect very minute effects. So while the emotional manipulation did have a statistically significant effect on posting behavior, it was an exceedingly minor one.

Part II

Affective Science in Action

3

BE THE SPARK

Crafting Your First (and Lasting) Impression

When I was twenty-two, fresh out of college and worn down to the nub working seventy-hour weeks in a poorly managed human services program I was desperate to leave, I interviewed for a research coordinator job at a local medical school. After interviewing with the doctors in charge of the program, I was introduced to the existing research coordinators. As I shook the hand of one of them, our eyes met and I was struck by the immediate conviction that should I join the research group, we would become inseparable. My actual thought at the time went along the lines of, *If I take this job, I'm going to fall head over heels for this woman.* While what followed was definitely less dramatic than that, it nonetheless has been and continues to be a friendship for the ages—starting with mix tapes and nights out dancing, then on to struggling together through matching doctoral programs, then to helping each other juggle the competing demands of motherhood and early careers.

Popular nonfiction writer Malcolm Gladwell tackled the unusual predictive power of experiences like this in his bestselling book *Blink: The Power of Thinking Without Thinking* (2007). The central premise—that we often make accurate judgments about people in the blink of an eye—grabbed the public's attention. The book was largely based on the psychological concept of thin-slicing, or the ability of people to use "thin slices" of behavior to predict more stable attributes. The concept is attributed to the brilliant (and dearly missed) social psychologist Nalini Ambady, who published a seminal paper on the topic with Robert Rosenthal (Ambady and Rosenthal, 1993). In one of her most famous studies on the topic, she asked research participants to watch brief videos of professors delivering lectures and then rate the characteristics of the professors (e.g., how enthusiastic, confident, and supportive they seemed). Ambady and Rosenthal then tested whether positive ratings on these characteristics could statistically predict the professors' actual end-of-semester evaluations from students—and they did, with surprising accuracy. Remarkably, not only did these evaluations successfully predict the ratings from students who spent the entire semester with these professors (attending their lectures, reading the texts they assigned, being graded by them, visiting them during office hours, and exchanging e-mails), but the videos lasted less than thirty seconds and *had no audio*. How could such a correlation between the two ratings be possible?

Ambady and Rosenthal ruled out the possibility that people were relying principally on physical attractiveness. They also didn't find strong contributions from specific nonverbal behaviors—for instance, the number of smiles in the videos of the professors. Rather, participants seemed to be relying on a more global overall impression based on a combination of multiple nonverbal behaviors.

To me this thin-slice research indicates two important points. First, the impression we make on our first days of class probably matters quite a bit. As John Steinbeck wrote in *East of Eden*, "People are felt rather than seen after the first few moments." On the first few days of class, students will be forming their impressions of you, and this impression may be more important than much of what you do later. Second, if perceived traits like optimism, confidence, and enthusiasm so effectively predict end-of-semester evaluations, anything we can do to maximize these traits in our teaching styles is probably going to yield positive outcomes. In other words, the nature of the content and activities you plan are important, but so is the style with which you present said content and activities. This matters not only for first impressions but also because when aiming for positive emotional contagion, enthusiasm and confidence are probably high on the list of affective states with beneficial effects.

While some people may use the fact that such superficial exposure could predict end-of-year teaching evaluations to critique teaching evaluations themselves as shallow popularity contests, I would argue first that it is not all that surprising that attributes like confidence, enthusiasm, and likability can be perceived in the briefest of exposures. Presumably these traits are conveyed through multiple nonverbal behaviors like posture, facial expressions, gestures, and degree of animation, and it may take only a few seconds for these attributes to be conveyed in such a way.

I would further argue that while warmth, confidence, enthusiasm, and likability are indeed elements of popularity, popularity may be something to aspire to. What is popularity, after all, other than being liked, admired, or supported by others? Being liked, admired, and supported by your students likely means that they are engaged, interested, and motivated to pursue shared goals. Certainly I agree with teaching evaluation detractors that one could waste this popularity-fueled enthusiasm and lead a class that doesn't engage the students' greater critical faculties— and perhaps some popular professors do. But I also firmly believe that someone who is liked, admired, and supported by his or her students will have a much better chance of leading those students to great heights of learning than one who is (if we simply flip the definition of "popular" on its head) disliked, disrespected, and opposed by students.

At the end of chapter 2 we considered the power of affective crossover, which would suggest that managing your own emotional state in a positive direction may light a fire under your students and lead to a more focused, enthusiastic classroom. In the rest of this chapter we'll consider some of the traits most predictive of teaching success in the thin slices study by Ambady and Rosenthal, and how one can embody these in the classroom. We'll consider these traits as good ways to maximize both a first impression on your first day of class and emotional contagion in subsequent classes.

Active and Enthusiastic

If at the front of the classroom you are not conveying enthusiasm for your material with at least a reasonable level of energy, how can you expect a class full of sleep-deprived, distracted students to eagerly tackle whatever you have planned? A list of all the good things sleep can do for your mental and physical well-being would exceed the pages of this chapter, but suffice it to say that people who are better rested perform better on almost any measure you can throw at them—from tasks of physical performance to mental acuity to the affective states they both feel and project outward.

In addition, at the end of this chapter we'll consider how just the act of managing your emotional impressions can tax your resources and make you tired. Starting out depleted will result in not only an unconvincing performance but also exhaustion.

Affective Crossover Teaching Practice 1: Practice Good Self-Care

The first thing you can do to maximize your daily effectiveness in the classroom is very straightforward and will have wonderful downstream effects on your health, productivity, and relationships—namely, take care of yourself. If you are sleep deprived and distracted by any number of concerns outside the classroom, this is likely to interfere with your ability to channel the energy required to teach enthusiastically. Thus, **get good rest and nutrition, exercise, and schedule regular downtime to decompress**. I tell my students every semester about research that indicates that studying for a few hours and getting a good night of sleep yields better exam grades than pulling an all-nighter. Similarly, your lecture (in the short term) and semester (in the long term) are likely to be of much higher quality if you spend extra time on self-care so that you can be energetic and enthusiastic than if you spend that same amount of time on extra lecture prep or killing yourself to return an assignment on time.

Every semester, I ask students in my Motivation and Emotion class to set a personal improvement goal for themselves; in subsequent weeks when we're considering research on goal-setting, motivation, and self-control, they apply these principles to the goals they set. One semester, about three years into my tenure track, I was grading a stack of these essays. I read essay after essay from students who had set exercise goals at the beginning of the semester, and while many of them had not met the specific—and often lofty—goals they set for themselves (e.g., "exercise every day"), the majority of them nonetheless maintained regular attendance at the gym. Meanwhile, I would start the semester intent on maintaining a variety of positive self-care behaviors, particularly regarding exercise. Yet semester after semester these self-care intentions would get shuttled to the side as the months progressed, ending with me inevitably bleary-eyed, soft of muscle, and swilling vats of coffee in an attempt to finish everything on time. I realized that my students were prioritizing their own self-care over putting extra work into our shared endeavors in the classroom, whereas I was responding to their lesser preparation and greater tiredness by pouring more of myself into a song-and-dance routine to grab their attention. I realized that this was an imbalance, and not a great example to set for them. Since that moment I have successfully avoided the midsemester exercise hiatus, and I openly discuss with them this realization and its effects when we talk about pursuing goals despite obstacles and overload in responsibilities.

Prioritizing self-care may be particularly important for both new faculty members on the tenure track (who have been plunked down in a new world of competing priorities, often in the absence of much guidance in terms of what success might look like) and for contingent faculty (who are often underpaid, undersupported, and juggling multiple jobs to make ends meet). Robert Boice (2000) has written extensively about the challenges facing new tenure-track faculty members and how to balance the multiple demands on one's time, and Richard Lyons (2004) has written about the same topics for adjunct faculty, including how institutions can better support their contingent faculty.

Life is life, and there will be some times when you'll have to fake energy or at least cover up your bedraggledness with some caffeine and undereye concealer, but do your best to be rested and fit. You'll be happier *and* a better teacher.

Besides being sure that you have the physical and mental resources to be fully engaged in your teaching despite the multiple demands on you, what are other ways you can portray and embody active, enthusiastic teaching? Two possibilities are through the employment of mindfulness and humor in your daily classes.

Mindfulness

In the 1970s Jon Kabat-Zinn devised a new application for meditation called mindfulness-based stress reduction at the University of Massachusetts Medical School. Relying on principles stemming from Buddhism, he defines mindfulness as "paying attention on purpose, in the present moment, and nonjudgmentally, to the unfolding of experience moment to moment" (Kabat-Zinn, 2003, p. 145). This training encourages people to enter into a state of mindfulness through a variety of practices including scanning the body for tension spots, yoga, focusing on the breath as a means of continually returning attention to the present moment, and accepting and then letting go of any self-judgmental thoughts. Mindfulness has been a topic of interest for the field of psychology since Kabat-Zinn launched the mindfulness movement in the 1970s, but in recent years there has been a veritable explosion of research, applications, and popular audience interest in the topic, leading *Time* magazine to launch a 2014 cover issue called "The Mindful Revolution."

What about mindfulness has engaged public interest to such a degree? For one, research has indicated a host of benefits from the regular practice of mindfulness, from boosting immune function to treating anxiety to curbing snacking. For another, huge, rapid advances in technology (smartphones! the quantified self! the Internet of things!) have led to predictable nervousness about the implications of this technology. People fret that because the technology is new, it must therefore be dangerous, and worry about the potential impact technology use might have on the quality of our relationships, our capacity for empathy, and—that eternal concern—the brains of our still-developing children. I suspect that part of the appeal of the mindful revolution—if you can call a resurgence of practices that can be traced back to the fourth century BCE a "revolution"—is that the doctrines of these age-old practices seem a natural antidote to the kinds of frenzied, technologically aided multitasking we are worried might be frying our brains. Try for a moment to imagine not responding to the demands currently pressing on you: a best friend texting you for relationship advice, a next-door neighbor hitting you up on Facebook to support her child's fund-raiser, or the sixty e-mails that have swarmed in over the time you've taken to read this chapter. Imagine instead just being in the present moment, feeling your breath cycle in and out of your chest in rhythmic waves, letting *I should be . . .* and *I should have . . .* float through your mind and then releasing these automatic thoughts without judging them or feeling their stickiness. Imagine actually smelling the heady aroma of a cup of coffee as you bring its warmth slowly to your lips, and actually listening to the crackle of the fire in the fireplace next to you. Sounds pretty good, doesn't it?

In sum, mindfulness feels wonderful, carries a host of medical and psychological benefits, and may be a cultural corrective to our mindless multitasking. But what does this all have to do with your classroom? If while you are teaching you are also mentally scrolling through the items you need to pick up at the grocery store on the way home, or internally responding to your reviewers' comments on your manuscript, you are unlikely to be conveying the same levels of active, enthusiastic connection with your students that you would if you were truly *there*. James Lang, author of *Cheating Lessons: Learning from Academic Dishonesty* (2013) and a regular contributor to the *Chronicle of Higher Education*, calls this a "pedagogy of presence" (Lang, 2015). He highlights the importance of teachers and students being present for one another in the process of learning—for teachers to be present and engaged in their instruction and (perhaps the bigger challenge) for students to be present and engaged in their participation in class activities and discussion. He asks: "While we stand up at the front talking, are students sitting out there in the seats, waiting for us to notice them and to step into their presence?"

This all makes good sense, but I'm a social scientist—do the data confirm this hunch that practicing mindful teaching might yield beneficial learning outcomes? This appears to be a topic of study that is just getting on its feet, but the early data are promising. First of all, there appears to be growing evidence that having students engage in activities informed by mindfulness yields benefits in learning and satisfaction. In a review of mindfulness practices in higher education, Mirabai Bush (2011), cofounder of the Center for Contemplative Mind in Society and coauthor with Ram Dass of *Compassion in Action: Setting Out on the Path of Service* (1991), details numerous examples of professors employing mindfulness directly in their classroom activities, in subjects as diverse as chemistry and gender studies. For instance, she notes that Michelle Francl, a professor of chemistry at Bryn Mawr College, trains all of her students in mindfulness practice because she feels that it will inform their exploration of science as a topic in both the classroom and in the field. "The world cries out for reflective scientists," Bush notes, "who can intentionally create a space in which to see their work in its full context—scientific, cultural, political, and personal." At Vassar College, professor Light Carruyo trains her students in mindfulness practice so that they can confront difficult issues such as structural inequalities without either being overwhelmed with emotion or needing to disregard the personal.

Researchers have also begun exploring how training teachers in mindfulness practices might inform their ability to lead meaningful classes on a variety of topics. Perhaps not surprisingly, since this research is so new, most of the studies have focused on elementary and secondary education rather than higher education. After all, one can imagine that the stress-reduction piece of mindfulness-based stress reduction (MBSR) would be a few orders of magnitude more relevant in classrooms where you can't rely on your students not to throw spitballs or pull each other's hair.

For instance, Maria Napoli (2004) studied three elementary school teachers trained in mindfulness over a year's time. The teachers reported that such training helped them to be present in the classroom, to focus their curriculum planning around decisions regarding core ideas and quality, rather than quantity, and to manage conflict in a peaceful and less stressed manner. In a similar design, Nirbhay Singh and colleagues (Singh, Lancioni, Winton, Karazsia, and Singh, 2013) enrolled three preschool teachers in an MBSR class and found that compared to the prestudy baseline, the children in these teachers' classrooms exhibited reductions in maladaptive behaviors such as challenging the teacher and engaging in negative social interactions. Without detailed research studies on the topic, we can't be sure of the mechanisms by which increased mindfulness in teachers could impact the maladaptive behaviors of students, but one might hypothesize that the mindfulness training led to teaching that was more present, clear, and positive, and that children in such classrooms were more relaxed and focused and less likely to act out. Putting these two studies together, it appears that training educators in mindfulness can yield benefits for the teachers, for classroom planning, and for student behavior.

While they are certainly interesting, both of these studies only examined a few teachers, and neither used a control group for comparison, so it is difficult to interpret their results too assuredly. In a gold-standard controlled study, Lisa Flook and colleagues (Flook, Goldberg, Pinger, Bonus, and Davidson, 2013) adapted an MBSR course specifically for teachers by changing the format slightly and including specific activities and practices related to school. They used a waiting list control design, in which half of the participants were studied while they waited to enroll in the MBSR class and half were studied during training. The variables they studied included levels of cortisol (a hormone known to be implicated in the stress response), ratings of psychological distress and burnout, responses on computerized tasks assessing emotion and cognition and, most important for our purposes, classroom behaviors. These behaviors were coded by trained coders blind to the study's hypotheses and the teacher's condition (current mindfulness or waitlist control). These classroom behaviors included *emotional support* (negative or positive climate in the classroom, teacher sensitivity to students, teacher respect for diverse perspectives), *classroom organization* (behavior management, classroom productivity, and instructional format), and *instructional support* (teacher assistance with problem solving, quality of feedback, etc.). The results were compelling, indicating significant changes following MBSR in psychological symptoms, self-compassion, and burnout. In addition, the teachers trained in mindfulness exhibited lower biases in attention toward emotion as well as improved classroom organization. In sum, the teachers were more satisfied with their work, better able to manage their attention to emotional matters, felt better, and conducted more organized classes. While additional studies are merited, and we need to examine whether these findings also apply to higher education, the early evidence seems clear: mindfulness may benefit everyone in the shared endeavor of education.

AFFECTIVE CROSSOVER TEACHING PRACTICE 2:
CONDUCT YOUR CLASSES MINDFULLY

The most straightforward aspect of mindfulness for teaching is a **continual calling back of attention to the present moment**. When you find yourself drifting off into thinking about what to make for dinner, or reciting facts or concepts by rote, stop yourself. Take a deep breath, and call yourself back to the present moment. One helpful technique is to make intentional eye contact with several students—to enter into the present moment with them. This calling back of attention is one of the most challenging aspects of mindfulness, but it is also one of the most important. It may feel difficult at first, and it may feel like a distraction from the flow of your teaching, but there are decades of research demonstrating that calling your attention back will become more natural over time.

Besides practicing this calling back of attention to the present moment, **being emotionally authentic** with yourself and with your students can also go a long way toward a more mindful, present classroom. In her book *Mindful Teaching and Teaching Mindfulness: A Guide for Anyone Who Teaches Anything*, Deborah Schoeberlein (Schoeberlein and Sheth, 2009) tells a story about teaching an HIV prevention class to urban adolescents while seven months pregnant. One of the students called attention to Schoeberlein's obvious pregnancy and questioned whether that meant that she had engaged in unprotected sex—the very behavior she was warning them against. While embarrassed and aware that the entire class was staring at her body and giggling at the girl's audacity, Schoeberlein intentionally employed mindfulness to be conscious of her own intense reaction and the class's titillated discomfort. She became present and attentive to these feelings. She deliberately took a deep breath and attempted to engage her emotions and the students thoughtfully, rather than reactively. She states:

> By switching my attention to my breathing and opening my awareness to what was happening, I could better manage my own emotions, reactions, and pedagogical response. Doing so positioned me to meet my students' needs and capitalize on this intense—and very teachable—moment. I didn't need to manage their behavior, because they shifted their attention and adjusted their own actions in response to my example. (p. xv)

With this more objective stance, she responded lightheartedly that yes, when attempting to have a child one does typically engage in unprotected sex. She then used the segue and the students' riveted attention to guide them to a discussion of healthy decisions as an adolescent leading to an adulthood with greater options.

Another way of being authentic and mindful is to **engage in metainstructing**—to call attention to the fact that an activity or assignment is not going well, and allow the students to take an active role in determining their instruction. In my Physiological Psychology course I once stopped midlecture and told my students that I could detect their nonengagement, and that I honestly could not differentiate between hopelessly lost and hopelessly bored and thus could not tell whether I should slow down or speed up. We discussed how they were feeling and it turned out that they were lost—I slowed down, backed up a few steps, and guided them back through the material.

Thus, don't just call your attention to the *what* of what is happening; pay attention also to the *how* (What are you currently feeling? What can you read or detect of the students' feelings?) and the *why* (What is the purpose of the current lecture or activity? Is your approach working or might a shift in gears be required?). If you are interested enough in mindfulness that you want something more thorough, **you can access some of the teacher-specific mindfulness elements included in Flook and colleagues' article (2013) in their appendix**. There are also numerous resources on mindfulness that you can access in written or audio format through online bookstores and other venues. Many schools and hospitals offer full classes in MBSR.

Humor

In addition to being mindfully engaged in the present moment, another route to an impression of active enthusiasm is through the use of humor. I'm not exactly known for my sense of humor, but luckily I'm not going to try to give you advice on how to be funny; instead I'm going to cite a bunch of facts and research studies, and then insert some notes of caution. Being a nerdy buzzkill is much more my strong suit.

The dominant theory of humor usage in the classroom is instructional humor processing theory (IHPT), proposed by Melissa Wanzer, Ann Frymier, and Jeffrey Irwin (2010), who argue that humor benefits instruction in two ways. The first should be no surprise to you after having read chapter 2—namely, that amusement is an affective state (and one that people quite enjoy) and, thus, using humor in the classroom is going to motivate, engage attention, hijack working memory, and yield memory consolidation benefits. Fair enough.

To explore the second way that humor benefits instruction according to IHPT, we need to unpack the what-makes-things-funny question a bit. The predominant theory of what makes things funny is the benign violation theory, most closely associated with Peter McGraw, researcher and coauthor with Joel Warner of the popular science book *The Humor Code* (2014). Essentially, McGraw, Warner, and other advocates of benign violation theory argue that something is funny when it violates your expectations—but in a harmless way. Another way to think about the violation aspect is through the notion of incongruity—you expect one thing, but then discover another. Someone slips and falls, but is not harmed; a child or small animal acts eerily like an adult or human; a joke leads you down one path, but then abruptly switches to another.[1]

The second reason humor benefits instruction is intrinsically tied into this violation/incongruity nature of humor. The IHPT argues that in the presence of humor, students detect and then have to resolve the incongruity between their original expectations and the humorous twist. This process of making one interpretation and then having to revise it results in a deeper level of mental processing than being exposed to the correct interpretation from the beginning; one is required to relate the information to more than one set of concepts and ideas, to reflect and elaborate on both the meaning of the initial interpretation and the revised interpretation. The level at which one processes information (called, most straightforwardly, the levels of processing theory) is one of the best predictors of successful memory recall.

Humor may thus benefit learning because mirth is an emotional experience with all its attendant benefits and because getting many academic jokes requires deep, elaborative processing. Could it be that humor also benefits learning through the effects of laughter? In a study that examined whether evoked mirth could benefit learning, Rana Esseily and colleagues (Esseily,

Rat-Fischer, Somogyi, O'Regan, and Fagard, 2015) asked a group of students to learn a task, and controlled whether the learning was humorous or not. But these were not college students; rather, they were eighteen-month-old children. The task was learning how to use a cardboard rake to reach a toy duck. All toddlers observed an adult using the tool for this purpose, but half of them observed a smiling adult in a simple demonstration and the other half observed a more humorous demonstration in which the experimenter jokingly threw the duck on the floor. The experimenters then studied which toddlers successfully used the rake to retrieve the duck when given their own turn. Intriguingly, the main difference wasn't between the toddlers in the straight versus the humorous conditions, but rather between the toddlers who laughed versus those who did not. Every toddler but one who laughed (93.7%) correctly used the rake to get the duck on the test trial, compared with a mere 25% of the humorous condition/nonlaughers and a measly 19% of the unfunny condition. It may be that this is a dose relationship, that a certain level of humor is required to benefit cognition, or it could be that there is something special about laughter (the physiological arousal perhaps?) that benefits learning and imitation. In any case, we don't know whether this study holds importance for our students, who are hopefully doing much more complicated things in our classes than retrieving plastic ducks, but it does point to a special role for humor in learning.

In sum, using humor might be an easy, enjoyable way to create a positive classroom environment and to engage students in a deeper, more elaborative processing of the course content.

Affective Crossover Teaching Practice 3: Include Accessible, Relevant Humor

Ronald Berk has performed much of the existing research on instructional humor. The first piece of advice he offers is that when deciding where and when to include humor, it can be a good idea to **take a top-down view of your class for the day, and see where it might be appropriate for a "commercial break" of humor** (Berk, 2014). Have you just completed a lecture on a complicated topic that required a great deal of focused attention from both you and your students? Slide in a joke about the material that requires students to apply the information they just learned to understand the joke. This joke would give everyone a bit of an emotional break from the seriousness of the material. You might also consider starting the class off with humor to encourage students' positive moods or remind them of the previous class's material, or you might end with humor to put a finishing touch on a topic.

John Banas, Norah Dunbar, Dariela Rodriguez, and Shr-Jie Liu (2011) reviewed four decades of literature on instructional humor in order to distill some common principles. First and foremost, their literature review revealed that for humor to work you need to **be sure that your students both detect the humorous incongruity and successfully resolve it.** If they don't, the result won't be positive emotion and greater understanding but instead negative emotion and decreased motivation. Nothing feels worse than a group of others laughing together at a joke that you don't have the knowledge to appreciate. For a first principle, then, don't use jokes that only experts in the field would understand. Or if you do, use the joke itself as an instructional exercise and unpack it with the class together. In my Introductory Psychology class, after discussing extensively how detecting a correlation or association between two variables tells you nothing about causation (because in the absence of a controlled experiment you can't tell whether X is causing Y, Y is causing X, or a third variable related to both is driving the relationship), I show my students a comic from Randall Munroe in which one friend tells another, "I used to think that correlation implied causation, but then I took a statistics class, and now I don't." The friend answers, "Sounds like the class helped." The first speaker then replies, "Maybe."[2] This joke is funny only if you have successfully mastered the idea that you can't draw cause-and-effect conclusions about the relationships between two variables, no matter how plausible the relationship is, without the existence of a controlled study.

The next principle is that the **humor should be relevant to the course**. If you're using humor to facilitate memory, you want to be sure that your students are remembering or processing material relevant to your learning goals rather than just a funny joke you happened to tell. Choose jokes or humorous lecture material that will nudge the students toward a deeper level of understanding.

Like any other human trait, the degree to which one is naturally funny varies a great deal. And unlike some other traits relevant to the classroom (you can, perhaps, fake your way into confidence or enthusiasm), humor cannot easily be forced or strategized. Thus, the next principle is to **never try to plan out humor that isn't natural, or become overly analytical or earnest about humor**. In graduate school I took a class on humor with affective scientist Reginald Adams, and he was fond of quoting E. B. White: "Analyzing humor is like dissecting a frog. Few people are interested and the frog dies of it." If humor doesn't come naturally to you, **be on the lookout for relevant humorous comics or video clips**, and allow other people to be funny for you.

Before we wrap up our humor advice, I'd like to issue a few cautionary statements about how delicate and complex it can be to decide which types and forms of humor to include. In recent years, we in higher education have developed a greater awareness of the importance of not only providing a fully inclusive environment for all of our students, but institutionalizing practices that ensure that our students perceive this inclusivity. This development is in many ways deeply vital and healthy. I'm sure we can all agree that we want all of our students to feel equally welcome and equally valued in our classrooms, and that we would never want anyone to feel marginalized on the basis of gender, race, ethnicity, sexual orientation, or any social grouping with which a person might identify. And indeed, humor can help in this regard: since much of humor relies on upending social norms, one can use humor to point out how many of our social norms are problematic, and how pervasive implicit attitudes about various groups are. For instance, cartoonist Liza Donnelly has made a career of penning cartoons for the *New Yorker* and other venues that ridicule some of the social norms we have about women and their roles in society.[3]

But the dark side of humor is that it can easily make problems of marginalization worse, for multiple possible reasons: because of poor choice of joke, because the varied experiences of your students mean only some of them understand the joke, or because you attempt to use a joke to point out the ridiculous nature of a marginalizing social norm but are taken to be in earnest by your students, who are then offended. Certainly none of us would want to create an unwelcome climate for any of our students.

On the other hand, in a viral (and contentious) article for the *Atlantic* called "The Coddling of the American Mind," Greg Lukianoff and Jonathan Haidt (2015) argue that our current generation of students is sheltered, quick to leap to offense, and unwilling to be confronted with viewpoints different from their own, and warn of the detrimental effects this perspective might have for both critical thinking and student well-being. In addition, there have been several high-profile cases of higher education lecturers and administrators whose positions have been terminated due to a perceived hostile culture for including jokes judged to be offensive by their students, and these developments certainly have some people worried. Kate Jeffrey, a behavioral neuroscientist at University College London, posted an entry on her blog titled "No More Jokes in My Lectures" in which she explained that because she delivers her lectures off the cuff and doesn't plan every sentence ahead of time in order to examine it for the various ways people could interpret (or misinterpret) her words, she feels too vulnerable in this atmosphere of intense scrutiny to continue to include jokes in her lectures:

> We are, as science communicators, placed in a very precarious position—we are supposed to deliver stand-up lectures in front of an audience with no notes, and make them interesting and entertaining (because we get judged by feedback afterwards) and we are also expected to allow anything about our lectures to be taped, tweeted or other released into the wild. Given modern social media this means that anything I say casually in a lecture might be stripped of its context, cast into the harsh glare of the internet spotlight and used to demolish me and my reputation. (Jeffrey, 2015)

This is a difficult enterprise. Beyond always **avoiding any sort of humor that traffics in stereotypes or prejudice** against any members of a social grouping, there are few easy recommendations when it comes to types of humor to include or avoid. To consider a few of the complexities, I would like to pose some questions followed by two contrasting answers.

First, should we always **employ culture-free** humor? If only some students understand your joke because of their age or where they grew up or what their primary language is, that's a problem. But at the same time, making jokes about culturally relevant trends or tropes can be a great way of developing rapport with your students, and also an easy way of making the information relevant to them.

What about **self-disparaging humor**? Used too often or in too extreme a form, self-disparaging humor can reduce student perceptions of your own credibility and confidence. Your students want to feel that you are a real human being with flaws, but they also want to feel that they are in the hands of a professional whom they can look up to and gain knowledge from. These risks of self-disparagement may be particularly salient if you possess other characteristics sadly implicitly associated in our society with lower power or credibility, such as if you're young for a professor, female, and/or a person of color. But on the other hand, self-disparaging humor, if used selectively and well, can be effective in that it can reduce student perceptions of the discrepancies in status and power between you and them. In turn, this may put them more at ease; your students may be more willing to risk being wrong in class discussions or while answering questions. It can also foster a sense of warmth and togetherness in the classroom.

Disparaging humor applied toward students, however, seems an easy no, right? You would never want to make fun of students for poor performance or an ill-thought-out contribution to class discussions. But then again, what about gentle teasing between professors and students who know each other well? Isn't gentle ribbing a part of the construction of close relationships?

I pose these two-sided complexities as important issues to consider when deciding what role, if any, humor has in your classes. I have no neat solutions or easy answers. Berk advises you to **have a colleague proof your slides or videos** to check for offensiveness, culture specificity, or simple lack of funniness. This may sound laborious, but given the universal enjoyability of humor, you may be surprised by how many of your friends and colleagues would be willing to watch a few funny clips on You-Tube for you. And given the current social climate, if you have any hesitations about how a joke might be perceived, it is likely well worth the investment of time and effort to get a second opinion.

Supportive and Warm

Support and warmth were also attributes that successfully pre-dicted end-of-semester positive evaluations in Ambady and Rosenthal's study. Thus, creating an impression of warm sup-port may be a good target for managing the emotional climate of your classroom. I'd like to believe that anyone getting up in front of a roomful of students with the aim of educating them would be supportive in those efforts, but these intentions may not be immediately apparent to your students. We human beings can be sort of miserable at understanding the world from each other's perspectives, especially when separated by things like maturity and expertise.

This point was driven home to me recently on a trip to Disney World with my daughter and my niece. We were wandering Epcot after dinner and stopped at a margarita stand for some liquid refreshments. While the adults conversed in line, the girls had my iPhone and were improvising a sweet song about the power of cousinhood that they were recording using the video app. We finished and paid, and I retrieved my phone. Later on, when I viewed the video, I was astonished to see the world through their perspective. The video was full of their faces and emotions and immediate concerns, and we adults were faceless, buzzing chatter coming from up high—mostly just background noise, once in a while issuing a command that came in clearer—or, at least, louder. At the end my hand and face suddenly swooped down from above like a pterodactyl as I retrieved the phone. I've so often had the experience of asking the children to do something specific, thinking I was being tremendously loud and clear, and then becoming very frustrated at having to repeat myself several times or explain what I just said. This thin slice of their world made me realize that *my* experience is not *their* experience—not by a long shot. Often they have trouble following commands not because they are being disobedient or recalcitrant (though they sometimes are those things too) but because the adult world and our demands are often obscure to them.

While our students are quite a bit older and closer to us in maturity and expertise than are my daughter and niece, we shouldn't forget that while we have been at this college-education thing for many a year (often decades), our students are still relative newbies. We have also been used to thinking from the top down about course content, reading books and blog posts on education, and debating in our departmental meetings about learning goals, assessment, and curricular reform. And that's all aside from our domain-specific knowledge: our understanding of the progression of ideas in our field, how they relate to each other, and current movements and trends. Our students have none of this expertise, and so what we are asking of them, and why and how it relates to their final grades in the course, are classroom dynamics that may be as fuzzy and higher up as my commands to the kids at Disney World.

Consider grades. I once had a heated disagreement with my much younger sister-in-law, who was in college at the same time as I was a junior faculty member. She was a great student, but she made some wry comments about how we professors had all the power and lorded it over the students. I asked her to clarify, and she specified that professors get to dole out *whatever grades they feel like*, and students (and their graduate school applications and future careers) were purely at our mercy. I spluttered for a bit in amazement. Putting aside the fact that all of my grading is done with explicit rubrics and Excel formulas and thus feels quite in the hands of the students and how much effort they apply, I protested that from my perspective, I was doing absolutely everything within my power to lead all of my students through a successful semester. These efforts vary from reading up on learning theory, to constantly revising lectures and exams to be more effective, to offering tips and strategies and review sessions wherever possible, and it seems to me that students practically need to apply effort to *not* succeed in my courses. That is my reality. Despite all this, however, students end up struggling and visiting me during office hours, protesting that they are doing everything in their power to succeed and applying all of the skills they have—skills that yield success in all other classes but mine. That is *their* reality.

Thus, spending some good time making yourself and your intentions as clear as possible to your students will do two important things: first, it will shore up their impression of you as a supportive instructor; second, it will increase your effectiveness as a teacher above and beyond their impressions of you. Clear communication and precise goals benefit any team enterprise. We'll consider much more closely some of the other benefits that various sorts of course clarity yield when we address increasing course clarity in order to decrease student anxiety in chapter 6.

Another route to warmth and transparency in the classroom is through instructor self-disclosure—that is, sharing yourself as a person with your students. In the classroom, self-disclosure could take the form of sharing anecdotes from your personal experiences, opinions on current events, or likes and dislikes. Sharing a bit of your personal self communicates to your students that the classroom is a safe place for sharing and that you are interested in being known and, in turn, knowing them. As David Gooblar, a teacher of literature and writing and author of the blog Pedagogy Unbound, writes,

> When you talk about yourself to your students you signal to them that you trust them and see them as worthy confidants. That, in turn, encourages students to feel more at ease, to open up themselves and commit more fully to the class. (2014)

Indeed, a wealth of literature on self-disclosure in personal relationships indicates that it is associated with a host of positive effects, including increased perception of closeness and intimacy, and positive evaluations of the discloser (Cayanus and Martin, 2008). Of course, instructor-student relationships are by definition professional ones, and thus should not be marked by the same level of intimacy that you'd expect in a more personal relationship.

Jacob Cayanus and Matthew Martin (2008) investigated student perceptions of teacher self-disclosure in a sample of 229 students in an introductory communications studies course. They used a self-developed self-report scale called, appropriately enough, the Teacher Self-Disclosure Scale, which included items assessing the frequency of disclosure (e.g., "My instructor often gives his/her opinions about current events"), the degree to which the disclosures were negative (e.g., "My instructor reveals undesirable things about him-/herself"), and the degree to which the disclosures were related or not related to course content (e.g., "My instructor provides personal explanations that make the content relevant"). They also assessed the students' affective evaluations of the course and instructor, their level of interest and motivation in the coursework, and the degree to which they felt their instructors were clear. The results revealed a pattern of associations whereby when students perceived their teachers as self-disclosing often and with little negativity, they also reported greater learning in the course and motivation to work hard and do well.

Instructor self-disclosure may thus be related to student interest and motivation, but does that come at a cost? Do students perceive the disclosing instructors as less credible or scholarly? Scott Myers and Maria Brann (2009) tackled this question in nine focus groups of undergraduate college students who reported on their perceptions of instructor self-disclosure and credibility. In this context, credibility is defined as the extent to which an instructor is thought to be trustworthy and believable and is characterized by three components: character (trustworthiness), caring (concern about student progress and welfare), and competence (perception of the instructor's knowledge). These focus groups revealed several themes. One was that self-disclosure often did enhance credibility. As one of their students put it,

> You'll have some instructors that don't open up or tell you anything about themselves and if you go to them after class you just don't really know how to relate to them or to kind of ask a certain question to them so when others that do relate to you, it makes you feel more comfortable. (Myers and Brann, 2009, p. 13)

The focus groups also revealed that students felt that self-disclosure, when relevant to the course material, is a method by which instructors demonstrate competence. These disclosures often took the form of sharing with the students how the instructor handled obstacles when first learning the material. One student elaborated on the credibility-enhancing power of self-disclosures by explaining that some instructors give the example in a PowerPoint presentation or notes and if the students don't understand the example, "that's it," whereas other instructors can easily relate the concept to a number of other personal examples: "I think that really shows that they have a foundation of information . . . being able to pull from other sources can demonstrate competence."

Notably, evaluations of credibility may be shifting as more socially connected generations enter the higher education classroom. Megan Gerhardt (2014) has evaluated both instructor and student rankings of contributors to teaching credibility and found that while both faculty and students rated competence in subject matter as the most important characteristic contributing to credibility and agreed that character was also highly important, students rated sociability (e.g., friendliness, warmth) as significantly more important than did faculty. Gerhardt speculates that as many students raised in the millennial generation in the United States have grown up with parenting and teaching styles that emphasize individual attention and team cohesion, they may enter the classroom with expectations of the same, and that "this desire for sociability has important implications for the classroom experiences of Millennials, reflecting the values of this generation and their desire for interaction, collaboration, relationships, and communication with their supervisors—in the classroom and beyond" (p. 12). Thus, being friendly and warm may be as important as being trustworthy and competent—or, looking at it another way, one route to being perceived as trustworthy and competent is to be friendly and warm.

AFFECTIVE CROSSOVER TEACHING PRACTICE 4: SELF-DISCLOSE (APPROPRIATELY) AND TELL STORIES

We already reviewed several of the principles regarding appropriate use of self-disclosure in the classroom as revealed by the student interviews, but to recap and expand a bit: **self-disclose, but do it selectively, and in ways that are relevant to the course material**. Students seem to respond most to self-disclosures that take the form of anecdotal examples of a phenomenon or concept (probably most relevant in disciplines like the social sciences) or expounding on how you strategized your way around difficult concepts or obstacles in your own process of learning. Don't self-disclose too frequently, don't self-disclose randomly, and don't self-disclose inappropriate information. Students do not need (or want) to hear about your drinking habits, your love life, or your squabbles with your department chair.

As I mentioned in the introduction to this book, we all have very different personas and teaching styles, and self-disclosure might not be your thing. You might prefer to maintain a perfectly professional demeanor and intellectual distance in the classroom, and that might work well for you. If so, or if you are looking for a way to vividly supplement your self-disclosures, you can include anecdotes and examples that don't necessarily pertain to your personal life. That is, you can **tell stories**.

Stories are like self-disclosures in that they provide context and meaning to information rather than presenting it in "vague abstractions" or "bulleted distillations" (Lowenthal, 2008). They also yield benefits in learning, because instead of the information being presented in discrete, isolated bits, each of which takes up its own slot in our working memory, it is presented as a holistic narrative tied together by meaning, which takes up much less of your working memory and also presumably relates in multiple ways to other threads of information stored in your long-term memory. Psychologists also believe that the causal elements (X event leads to Y consequences), the presence of social characters with motivations, and the adherence to certain narrative structures similarly yield benefits to comprehension (Willingham, 2004).

Moreover, if you are looking to introduce a little emotional punch to a lecture or assignment, stories are a great route to emotion. In a blog post, popular author Paul Zak tells a story of watching the film *Million Dollar Baby* on an airplane and disintegrating into sobs despite the reassurances and concern of his fellow passengers. He calls our attention to the fact that he was in full possession of his capacities, fully aware of the societal expectations regarding emotional composure in public places, and yet unable to stop the flow of tears. Stories mentally transport us into the lived moments of another human being. Perhaps not terribly surprisingly, this transportation of our minds is reflected in changes in our brain activity when we're exposed to stories. It turns out that when you watch someone's brain while they read a story, you can virtually watch the story unfold according to which areas of the brain are activated (Speer, Reynolds, Swallow, and Zacks, 2009). When the characters pick up a spoon, you see activity in the areas of the brain involved in grasping objects. When they navigate a spatial terrain, areas involved in spatial navigation light up. To the brain, stories are miniature experiences.

Thus, rather than simply sharing a scientific theorem or mathematical concept, tell also the story of its discoverer and how he or she worked through the process of discovery. Poet Kathleen Quinlan suggests that by discussing the scholars behind the work you're presenting as real people living and working within a particular time period, you lead students to the thought that they also could contribute such knowledge: "By putting students into relationship with the subject and its key authors and ideas, we are inviting them to join this community of scholars and sending the message that they, too, can become authors of their own ideas" (2016, p. 3).

Examples in which scholars had to overcome adversity or writer's block, or discovered the solution in their sleep, are easily found and should be included. Wherever possible, include profiles of scholars of diverse backgrounds so that all students see role models with whom they identify. Hollywood is rather in love with biopics at the moment, and so you could start a topic by watching the movie trailer for a film about the discoverer. If you're teaching a social science, take a page from a politician's playbook. How many times have you heard an American presidential hopeful use a vivid anecdote of a struggling single mother or small business owner to illustrate the effects of the other party's poor economic policies? Or you could illustrate the nature of a certain mental illness by pulling from a casebook of anonymized accounts of real patients struggling with real symptoms. If you're teaching history or literature, the work is already there for you: your very subject matter is stories.

Stories convey interest and enthusiasm and may be "psychologically privileged" (Willingham, 2004) in terms of memory. Whether they're your own, other people's, or fictionalized, tell stories.

Confident and Optimistic

In Ambady and Rosenthal's study, the two attributes most highly predictive of positive end-of-year evaluations were confidence and optimism.

Confidence

A quote that makes the rounds in my Twittersphere every now and again goes something like, "The secret to successful teaching is pretending like you've always known something you learned just this morning." There are two things I'd like to consider about this quote. The first is that embedded within the meaning of the quote is the implicit understanding that the confidence with which you present your knowledge and your topic of study goes quite a long way to a successful imparting of knowledge, regardless of your pre-existing competence or skill.

Second, while hopefully you were hired to teach a course because you do possess a certain level of expertise in the subject matter, it is also impossible to know everything there is to know about a particular topic, especially if you are teaching a broad survey course in your discipline. Moreover, in most fields there are new and exciting developments occurring all of the time that deserve a front row seat in your lectures, and so you may want to include a new topic of study or research technique that you literally did learn about just this morning (Huston, 2009).

There are other routes to portraying confidence beyond putting on a good game face and delivering the material with conviction. Given the dyadic nature of human social relationships, you will feel more confident if students view you as a credible authority. But how do you manage this impression? Recall from our coverage of being supportive and warm that students' perceptions of teacher credibility seem to be tied up in their evaluations of your degree of character, caring, and competence. Because character (trustworthiness) and caring are all wrapped up in being supportive and warm with your students, and we just covered that, let's now tackle competence.

The most straightforward road to perceived competence is knowing what you're talking about—having a solid base in your discipline. Let's presume that that's generally the case. Let's also presume that you know that the more prepared you are for a lecture, the more you've read about and thought about the material, the more you've anticipated student questions and investigated them, then the more competent you will seem—for the simple reason that you'll *be* more competent.

Good classroom management is also likely to impact perceived competence. In higher education we typically have the luxury of not worrying about the same challenges to classroom management that, say, our friends who teach in elementary or secondary school have. After all, our students are there voluntarily, are legal adults who have learned how to comport themselves in a classroom, and have passed a certain threshold of behavior and achievement in order to gain admittance to the institution. There are, however, still certain rules one needs to decide whether to enforce, and how one does so may impact student perceptions of your credibility. For instance, I'm sure we all know stories about professors who insist on punctuality to the extent that they lock the door or otherwise bar late entries, or those who will stop a lecture and wait quietly if people start packing up early. Probably the most common classroom management issue that confronts modern higher education instructors is what to do about all of the digital distractions. More students than not these days have smartphones, with all of their attendant possible distractions—social media, games, and the Internet. Even those without smartphones have mobile phones capable of texting, and today's whippersnappers spend an inordinate amount of time texting (or whatever has replaced texting in the time elapsed between my writing this and you reading it). Smartphones aside, many students often ask permission to use their laptops or tablets to take notes. What does one do about it all?

Amber Finn and Andrew Ledbetter (2013) investigated the relationship between teacher technology policies and perceived credibility of teachers in a few hundred undergraduate communications students. They evaluated three possible policies regarding technology use in the classroom: encouraging, discouraging, and laissez-faire. They found that students expected to be able to use their wireless devices in the classroom, and that teachers who encouraged such use were rated as more credible across all three dimensions (character, caring, and competence). Notably, these encouraging policies were associated with teachers utilizing technology in the classroom as well, perhaps by having students access answers to questions using their devices or accessing course materials on a course management website. In other words, instructors who are technologically proficient and who encourage students to use technology tend to be one and the same, so we can't know whether the good ratings are related to the former or the latter (or both, or to a third variable like youth).

In supplementary findings, Finn and Ledbetter discovered that being clear about one's policy was associated with credibility regardless of what the policy was; they thus encourage instructors interested in using a discouraging policy to consider ways in which they could discourage technology use while maintaining credibility by being clear about the parameters of the policy but—even more important—explaining *why* such a policy has been chosen. For instance, you could draw on a series of recent studies demonstrating that students who take notes in longhand rather than on a digital device demonstrate better learning (e.g., Mueller and Oppenheimer, 2014). You could also offer a reward in return for what the students may see as a punitive measure. I experimented with a laptop ban in my classes this semester, and I combined these two suggestions—I explained the *why* using the studies I just cited, and I offered to post all of my slides online the night before class so that students could download them and have them to take notes on. What Finn and Ledbetter's study suggests most strongly is that to maintain credibility, one needs to adopt a technology policy and explain it clearly; an unexplained, laissez-faire approach benefits no one.

AFFECTIVE CROSSOVER TEACHING PRACTICE 5: BE CREDIBLE, CONFIDENT, AND COMPETENT

Recall that your students' perceptions of how credible you are is made up of perceptions of your trustworthiness, your degree of caring, and your level of competence. So *be* these things! Follow through on your word. While you want your syllabus to be an invitation to learning, you also want it to be clear and informative. Whenever possible, **treat the syllabus as if it's a contract, then stick to it**. When I overhear students complaining about perceived injustices on the part of professors (and yes, I realize they might just as easily be gossiping about *me* in *your* classes), it is most often due to a sense of untrustworthiness or unreliability of various sorts: "He said the paper would be graded on X, and then he graded on Y!" or, "She said we were only going to have three writing assignments, and then halfway through the semester decided to add three more!" Obviously you want to build some flexibility into your syllabus so as to be able to nimbly respond to unexpected changes in course schedules (record-breaking winter of 2014–15 in New England, I'm looking at you) or the discovery of new materials, but wherever possible, strive for clarity and avoid the sudden addition of extra work or unexpected due dates.

In chapter 6 we'll examine how clarity in course assignments and grading rubrics can have a huge dampening effect on anxiety, but for now it is worth noting that being as transparent as you possibly can about your motivation in assigning certain tasks, what the work of the semester will entail, and how grades will be determined will all also enhance your students' perceptions of your credibility. As we discussed, also **make decisions about which rules you will and won't enforce ahead of time** (e.g., your policy on classroom technology use), state these clearly up front, and then follow through with them.

Caring can be demonstrated through simple warmth, through some immediacy cues like eye contact and smiling, and by taking the time to frequently check in with student progress. **Pause in your coverage of a certain block of material or technique to ask if there are any questions or, even better, distribute surveys or quick assessments of perceived understanding**. These techniques can go a long way in demonstrating that you care deeply about students' progress. Frequently on my end-of-semester course evaluations, students will mention appreciating that I conducted midsemester evaluations—even in those semesters when I don't actually make any changes to my teaching practices based on such evaluations! The perception that I care about how things are going is seemingly enough to benefit their perception of my credibility.

Finally, be competent. **Know your material, prepare well, and only agree to teach courses that you feel you have a decent level of mastery in**. Also, no teacher can know all the ins and outs of an entire field. If students ask questions you don't know the answer to, don't fake it—let them know you'll investigate the answers before the next class, and then follow through.

Beyond being competent, demonstrate your confidence in your competence by presenting the material with conviction, the assumption that that your audience will be interested, and energy.

Optimism

Melanie Tannenbaum is a social psychologist and the author of the very successful PsySociety blog at Scientific American. In one blog post, she mentions that she is also a Zumba instructor; she draws several analogies between teaching her Zumba classes and writing about science, but the one that strikes me is her third reflection—that by the time you are sick of something, your audience is probably just getting into it:

> Don't underestimate the interest level of your audience. Don't assume people are bored with what you have to say, or that they moved on to caring about other topics. You really might be surprised by how long people will stay interested in something that you tired out on a while ago. (Tannenbaum, 2015)

This is another way in which we have difficulty understanding the mental worlds of other people—particularly our students. When you have been mired in a subject for decades, it can seem like the most complicated things are very simple. This interferes with good teaching, because if you can't recall why and how a particular topic can be difficult it becomes much harder to break it down for new learners, as well as to identify ahead of time where they might get stuck and strategize ways to make those areas clearer. I've seen this in my own teaching evolution. While in certain ways I have clearly improved as an instructor as I have gained more experience and learned more about pedagogy, I worry also that my ability to break really complicated matters down and understand why students aren't grasping the subject matter is slipping. My course evaluations are usually quite good, but one student from my introductory neuroscience class recently wrote something along the lines of, "There are really smart people who can still communicate with people who aren't experts. Sarah Cavanagh is not one of them." Ouch!

But beyond the expertise issue, Tannenbaum also taps into something related to optimism and energy. This is probably particularly true of her Zumba instruction; if she assumes that her audience is as bored of the routine as she is, her presentation is going to exhibit that boredom and her class is probably going to respond with a low level of enthusiasm. If, however, she taps into her initial excitement about the new routine (or, by extension, a new science topic) and portrays that, perhaps by recalling that she has the privilege of sharing this new information with the class, her energy and positive emotions will demonstrate that and be infectious. Her interest will stimulate her students' interest.

Thus, one path to portraying optimism is assuming that your students will be interested and presenting the material as if it is as newly fascinating as when you first discovered it. What about other forms of optimism? Angela Lee Duckworth is a researcher who first spent several years teaching high school, then went back to graduate school for her doctorate and now teaches at the University of Pennsylvania. She and some colleagues (Duckworth, Quinn, and Seligman, 2009) took a look at the predictors of excellent precollege teaching and found that the literature was hopelessly confounded—for instance, the best teachers tend to get a number of job offers and can choose jobs in higher-paying, higher-performing school districts. In another example, teaching effectiveness is often measured by student or peer ratings, which can be more based on other positive attributes (e.g., extraversion or social competence) and don't necessarily reflect student learning.

To avoid some of these methodological tangles, Duckworth and her colleagues studied students volunteering in the Teach for

America (TFA) program, which matches high-performing new teachers with underperforming schools across the nation. Students in this program don't have a choice of placement, they face frequent challenges, and built into the program are assessments of learning and mastery of content. The variables Duckworth and colleagues chose as possible predictors of learning were "grit" (tenacity in goal pursuit in the face of obstacles), life satisfaction (the hypothesis that children might learn better from people who project happiness and energy in the classroom), and optimistic explanatory style. This last variable measures how you explain the causes of emotional events in your life; whether you attribute the cause of the event to be more temporary or more stable (e.g., *This romantic rejection is a single occurrence*, versus *I will always fail at love*) and more specific or more global (e.g., *This course failure means I am bad at physics*, versus *I am unintelligent*). People high in optimistic explanatory style explain negative events to themselves as temporary and specific and positive events as stable and global. Notably, this was a longitudinal study—that is, Duckworth, Quinn, and Seligman assessed personality measures before students began teaching, and the effectiveness (TFA's ranking of the teachers based on the academic gains of their students) was measured at the end of the year. This design eliminated the possibility that teachers who had had a successful teaching year reported being more gritty and optimistic—and vice versa. Their preexisting ratings predicted how the teaching would go.

The results confirmed the authors' suspicions. All three variables (grit, life satisfaction, and optimistic explanatory style) predicted teaching effectiveness in the form of students who were performing better and accomplishing greater academic gains. Life satisfaction was the strongest predictor. The authors speculate that this may be because happier people create a happier classroom climate, and that this leads to academic gains. They quote from Harold Lyon on first-year teaching:

> These young children needed help with reading and mathematics, but they also needed much more in their lives. They needed imagination and self-confidence. So we sang, happily and frequently. We recited, clapped, danced, and wiggled. We explored sounds and ideas. We discussed issues and concerns. We drew pictures and made up songs and stories, injecting into the grimness of many of their lives small pockets of joy. I could feel the love growing between us. (Charles, 1991, quoted in Duckworth et al., 2009, p. 545)

While we are less likely to be wiggling and coloring in the higher education classroom and we need experimental studies assessing these relationships in the context of higher education, I think the point nonetheless stands: happier, more optimistic teachers could lead to greater academic gains in students.

Affective Crossover Teaching Practice 6: Be Optimistic, Portray Immediacy

You may have read the section on portraying interest and optimism and positive emotions and thought to yourself, *Well, that's all great in terms of general principles, but what does interest and optimism look like?* That is, how can you demonstrate your own positive emotions in such a way as to inspire similar emotions in your students?

I propose two practices. The first is focusing on the degree to which your verbal and nonverbal behaviors are demonstrating immediacy. Related to being mindfully in the moment and connected with your students, immediacy pertains to behaviors that are both spoken and unspoken and convey to students that you are interested in them, the material, and the process of learning. In terms of verbal behavior, immediacy consists of some of the behaviors we've already discussed, such as implementing humor and self-disclosure. It also consists of **complimenting students for good contributions and using inclusive pronouns** ("Next, we are going to discuss together . . ." versus, "Next I'm going to have you discuss . . .").

Nonverbal immediacy is demonstrated through **eye contact, leaning forward, smiling, a relaxed posture, use of gestures, a variety of vocal tones, and movement around the classroom**. If you have ever attended a conference talk where the speaker stood stock-still behind the podium and read off notes or slides without making eye contact or varying his or her tone, you are familiar with how necessary nonverbal immediacy behaviors are for a good presentation. You may also reflect that presentations of this sort, even if they are only ten or fifteen minutes long, seem to be utterly interminable. Imagine then being subjected to hours of such presentations, several times a week for fifteen weeks or so. Don't do that to your students—not just because it is unlikely to translate into learning, but also because it is cruel.

I don't think we need a big research study to demonstrate that classes led with verbal and nonverbal immediacy are more pleasurable and attention grabbing than those led without them. But what about learning? Paul Witt, Lawrence Wheeless, and Mike Allen (2004) conducted a meta-analysis of several decades of literature (over eighty studies) on the topic.[4] Their findings revealed that verbal and nonverbal immediacy were both significantly associated with students' perceptions of how much they had learned, their ratings of how much they liked the course and/or the instructor, and how likely they thought it was that they would pursue future learning in the given domain. For those studies that attempted to measure actual learning in various ways (e.g., course grades, test scores, etc.), immediacy of both sorts was also associated with greater learning, though these effects were noticeably weaker than for perceived affective learning. Of course, all of this is correlational (teachers weren't randomly assigned to use high or low immediacy), and immediacy could be confounded with any number of other variables we've already considered (mindfulness, humor, energy, choice of activities, etc.). But it can't hurt. And, **smile!** Smiling is both an immediacy cue and a known inducer of positive mood states and a signal of affiliation and approval.

To increase immediacy in your teaching, it is probably most effective to **try increasing one or two of these behaviors at a time**. Otherwise you might be so distracted by your self-monitoring that you are behaving in a strange or stilted way or unable to focus on conveying the course material clearly. One week make a real effort to make more eye contact, and do so until you are comfortable and in the habit of doing so. Then try to change your movement: nudge yourself into more movement by using the whiteboard or leaving your water bottle on the opposite side of the room. Getting a colleague to **videotape a few of your lectures** can be terrifying but extremely edifying, and it's likely you'll find that you are already engaging in some of these immediacy behaviors and thus can target the ones that are missing.

The second practice for portraying interest and optimism is quite simply to teach things that you are interested in and optimistic about. Granted, there are always limits on what you have to cover in a certain course, but there are usually also a lot of choices involved. **Teach what you love, and if you find your interest in a given topic or book or research study flagging and your presentation of it becoming rote, mix it up with a**

new one. Beyond practicing immediacy during delivery, actually tell the students you are deeply interested in and curious
about the material. Researchers have demonstrated that the
mere act of telling students that their instructor was there on a
volunteer versus paid basis led to greater motivation and performance (Radel, Sarrazin, Legrain, and Wild, 2010), presumably
because students extrapolate the interest of the volunteer and
thus become more interested themselves. Stopping your lecture
midstream to exclaim your natural enthusiasm can give everyone a little boost.

A Note on Faking It

Thus far in this chapter we have assumed that quite at will, you
can bring into being sparkling experiences of enthusiasm, amusement, optimism, confidence, and immediacy. At times you may
be able to do just that. I have also suggested that you should
intentionally choose to discuss topics and readings that engender
these experiences naturally within yourself. It is unlikely, however, that many of us can maintain such states day in and day
out, yet we may still want to harness the power they hold. Let's
evaluate whether there is value in *faking it*—in putting on an
enthusiastic, optimistic outer appearance when inside you might
be feeling anything but.

   To begin our examination of the value of artificially display-
ing or hiding emotions versus maintaining authenticity in the
classroom, I'd like you to consider clowns. Judging from a quick
Google search, if your reaction to thinking about clowns is
anywhere on the negative side of the spectrum (from mild dis-
like to full-blown phobia), you're far from alone. It might make

an interesting tangent to ponder just what is so creepy about clowns, but what I'd actually like to consider right now is how it might feel to be one. Even putting aside the fact that you're wearing a heavy costume festooned with all manner of crinkly, puffed-up bits and slathered in thick makeup that dries to a tight, pasty sheen locked to your face and neck, you have to act jolly and overexuberant for hours on end, whether or not you've gotten enough sleep last night, whether or not you got in a fight with your girlfriend right before the event *and* are coming down with the flu, and whether the crowd you've been hired to entertain is in a friendly mood or they're actually made up of a bunch of clown-o-phobes like me.

Exhausting, right?

I hate to break it to you, but if you are a teacher, you are a sort of clown. While constant elation and glee isn't required, you almost definitely are engaging in some management of whether or not you express your sincere emotions, whether that management takes the form of counterfeiting eagerness to give a lecture or hiding your irritation with the student who continually challenges you on every grade point. Even beyond the desire to portray affective states that will engender student interest and motivation, we teachers have to follow certain social rules about the emotions that are appropriate to display: we are supposed to remain calm, treat the go-getter in the front row with the same degree of positivity and goodwill as the surly sleeper in the back row, and maintain a generally professional demeanor. These unspoken social guidelines for behavior for a given role in a given social situation are known as display rules, and the display rules for a teacher in a classroom are pretty strict.

When you mask your true emotions in order to perform your job, organizational psychologists call this surface acting. As it turns out, hiding your true emotions is sort of exhausting. To surface act, your brain uses up resources like attention and working memory, and as we know, these resources are limited. When you inhibit your natural reactions, you must engage in three different stages of effort: first, you need to make the decision and "act of will" to control your expressions and body language; second, you need to engage all of the behaviors and physiology to make this a reality (smooth your brow, smile, take a deep breath); and third, you need to keep track of how successful you are being, whether you should switch gears, and so on. This whole process may be quite tiring, and your awareness of how tiring it all is can make it that much worse. This is why the overarching term that considers both surface acting and other forms of emotional management in the workplace is *emotional labor*, because that's just what it feels like—labor.

To examine emotional labor in the classroom, Jamie Taxer and Anne Frenzel (2015) of the University of Munich evaluated a group of secondary school teachers and assessed both their hidden emotions (which were more likely to be negative emotions like frustration or anger) and their surface emotions (which were more likely to be positive affective experiences like enthusiasm or excitement) and the relations of each to a number of teacher variables. The first question they addressed was how frequently teachers engage in the practice of hiding or faking emotions in the classroom, and they found that indeed, these practices were quite frequent. Teachers reported both faking unfelt positive emotions and hiding felt negative emotions between "a few times a month" to "a few times a week." They reported more frequently expressing genuine, felt positive emotions (on the order of a few times per class) and rarely ever expressing genuine, felt negative emotions (between "never" and "a few times per month"; in terms of specific negative emotions, disappointment was the most frequently expressed negative emotion).

In sum, these teachers reported managing their displays of both positive and negative emotions, presumably to encourage student interest and manage the emotional climate of the classroom. But of course, not all teachers reported doing so to the same degree, so the next question Taxer and Frenzel tackled was the degree to which doing so was more or less associated with aspects of the teachers' well-being and satisfaction with their classroom experiences. They found that

> teachers who reported frequently genuinely expressing their positive emotions were efficacious, felt related to their students, were mentally healthy, satisfied with their jobs, and had low levels of emotional exhaustion, whereas teachers who reported frequently genuinely expressing their negative emotions had low teaching self-efficacy beliefs, poor mental and physical health, were emotionally exhausted and unsatisfied with their jobs. (Taxer and Frenzel, 2015, p. 85)

In other words, genuinely expressing positivity was associated with all sorts of good experiences in and out of the classroom, and genuinely expressing negativity was associated with bad experiences.

These results are certainly interesting, and in sum they reaffirm the sense that in the classroom, positive is good and negative is bad. But two cautionary notes are in order: first, these data are all correlational; second, they are all based on the teachers' reflections of their own behaviors and experiences. Happy people almost by definition have higher well-being, energy, and more positive emotions than unhappy people, and also are likely to rate all sorts of aspects of their life more positively. They might not actually be better teachers—they may just *think* they are. Or the happiness might come first and contribute to both more positive emotions expressed in the classroom and better teaching: they might be better teachers because they're happy, not happy because they're better teachers. There is no way using a correlational research design can disentangle these possibilities.

In terms of faked and hidden emotions, both types of regulating were associated with poor health and emotional exhaustion, a finding echoed in a study by Melanie Keller and colleagues (Keller, Goetz, Becker, Morger, and Hensley, 2014). These researchers explored the interactions of emotional labor and emotional exhaustion in secondary school teachers over a two-week period using experience-sampling methodology, where handheld devices periodically prompted the teachers to report on their current experiences. The teachers reported frequently feeling enjoyment (99% of lessons) and anger (39% of lessons). The teachers reported either faking or hiding their emotions for about one-third of all of their lessons. Perhaps unsurprisingly, feeling emotionally exhausted was linked with lower feelings of enjoyment and greater feelings of anger, and greater feelings of anger were linked with greater application of emotional labor. The authors point to the possibility that future studies should evaluate whether increasing enjoyment in the classroom might reduce both the need for emotional labor and, correspondingly, help prevent emotional exhaustion and (eventually) burnout.

Neither of these studies evaluated student learning or student satisfaction with the teacher or the course. We mentioned earlier in the book that sometimes negative moods can make you more accurate than positive moods; could something similar be true of teaching and learning as well? Might you learn more from the curmudgeonly taskmaster than from the reassuring idealist? Evert van Doorn, Gerben van Kleef, and Joop van der Pligt (2014) set out to test this hypothesis. They posit that one might learn more from a critical instructor because happiness and positivity are signals that all is well and behavior does not need to change, whereas negative emotions like anger are signals that behavior must shift in order to bring it in line with expectations. Presumably, shifting behavior in line with teacher expectations is part of active learning, and thus receiving negative feedback from an instructor might be associated with better learning.

In their experiment, college undergraduates were presented with a word task to learn and then were tested for baseline performance. These scores were sent to an "instructor" (in reality, an actor) who then delivered some study tips in either an angry or a happy way (including changes in vocal tone, gestures, etc.). The students were sent home with the study tips and instructed to study them at least five minutes a day, because at the end of the week they would return for a follow-up test. Van Doorn and colleagues found that the students whose baseline performance was followed by study tips delivered in an angry tone outperformed those whose study tips were delivered in a happy tone. Notably, participants did not report feeling more negative or fewer positive emotions under the angry versus the happy condition, suggesting that this effect was not due to an impact on the students' emotional experiences; rather, it was the informational value of the angry tone that seemed to be important. The angry tone conveyed the information that the students' performance left something to be desired, and this presumably affected their studying behavior over the week and yielded good learning outcomes. Though it was a small, preliminary study, this work indicates that there may be a place for expressing some negativity in the classroom, at least in response to lower-than-expected performance on assessments. As always, context and tone are probably important. Some well-placed disappointment after the bulk of the class performs undesirably on an assessment is more appropriate and likely more effective than a temper tantrum about poor performance.

Evaluating this literature in sum, it seems that the weight of the data lies with emotional authenticity; emotional labor is exhausting, and emotional exhaustion may be linked with greater anger, which may then require more emotional labor to hide it! Moreover, at least one study (van Doorn, van Kleef, and van der Pligt, 2014) indicates that giving performance feedback in a frustrated tone may occasionally spur better performance. While most of this work is correlational, and thus it is difficult to make firm recommendations at this juncture, it seems to me that the safest bet is where we started: wherever possible, instead of trying to fake interest and enthusiasm in tired or boring material, do what you can to teach activities and topics and assignments that genuinely interest you.

Chapter Summary

At the end of chapter 2 we reviewed how powerful the forces of emotional contagion and affective crossover can be in the classroom, and in this chapter we took a closer look at which instructor attributes will lead to the best sorts of contagious emotions. In some ways, managing the emotional climate of your classroom is the most powerful step you can take to maximizing your students' attention and motivation, which we know are the critical first steps to learning. As Mary Helen Immordino-Yang and

Antonio Damasio state, "When educators fail to appreciate the importance of students' emotions, they fail to appreciate a critical force in students' learning. One could argue, in fact, that they fail to appreciate the very reason that students learn at all" (2007, p. 9). Much like how all of your own goals and tasks seem so much more interesting and achievable on a sunny, lilac-filled morning in May than on a dark, sleety morning in March, so too will your students be more energetic and interested if the person at the front of the classroom is engaged, funny, confident, positive, and supportive. Be the change you wish to see in them.

Further Reading

For more details on **thin slices**, see Ambady, Nalini, and Skowronski, John J. 2008. *First impressions.* New York: Guilford Press.

For the seminal work on **mindfulness-based stress reduction**, see Kabat-Zinn, Jon. 1990. *Full catastrophe living: Using the wisdom of your body and mind to face stress, pain, and illness.* Delacorte, NY: Delta.

If you are stuck **teaching a course on a topic that is entirely new to you**, but you still want to seem confident, see Huston, Therese. 2009. *Teaching what you don't know.* Cambridge, MA: Harvard University Press.

For more evidence that **immediacy is an important determinant of student learning**, see Witt, Paul L., Wheeless, Lawrence R., and Allen, Mike. 2004. A meta-analytical review of the relationship between teacher immediacy and student learning. *Communication Monographs, 71*(2), 184–207. doi:10.1080/036452042000228054

NOTES

1. Two hunters are out in the woods when one collapses. The second guy whips out his phone and dials 911, saying, "My friend collapsed, and I think he's dead! What should I do?" The emergency operator responds, "Calm down. First, let's make sure he is really dead." There is a silence, and then a gunshot is heard. Back on the phone, the guy says, "Okay, now what?"

2. For more of Munroe's comics, see http://xkcd.com.

3. In one, two little girls are playing with dolls, and one is saying to the other, "I haven't decided what I'll be when I grow up—a good girl or a slut."

4. Meta-analysis is a powerful statistical technique that allows one to test the strength of an effect across many different studies.

4

BURNING TO MASTER

Mobilizing Student Efforts

Every academic major has its dreaded courses: the sudden bitter bite of fruit peel in the middle of a sweet hot cross bun. Premed students moan about the seemingly impossible "orgo"—organic chemistry. Literature students groan about lit theory. For psychology majors, the most frequent complaints are about their statistics requirements. More often than not, students are attracted to psychology because they want to eventually occupy the psychotherapist's chair, or because they want to advise police detectives on how to find serial killers. Few psychology students are excited at the prospect of learning statistics, and many of them actively resent it. If we're to consider best practices in mobilizing students' efforts and getting them focused and interested in the material at hand, there is probably no more challenging venue for doing so in psychology than a statistics classroom.

Psychologist Jennifer DiCorcia has delighted numerous classrooms of unsuspecting psychology majors with her fresh infusion of humor and intellectual challenge into this dry topic. One of the statistical concepts she teaches is called multiple regression, and it involves predicting outcomes based on other known measurements. For instance, you might try to predict final course grades using midterm grades and hours spent studying, or weight loss using calories consumed and hours exercised in a week. Statistics classes typically involve learning the rationale for the test, then practicing examples with a lot of numbers. Students who don't enjoy math tend to find these problems extremely dull, and the class tends to drag on.

To teach linear regression, DiCorcia implements an activity called Bungee Jumping Barbie.[1] She breaks the class into small groups and tells them each they are an extreme sporting company and that Barbie is a celebrity client with a taste for adrenaline. Barbie wants to hire the company that can give her the most thrilling, death-defying bungee jump yet . . . without risking her life and limb. DiCorcia gives each group the previous data on each of Barbie's test jumps—how long the rope was and how far she dropped. The students use the data to calculate the appropriate statistics, and tend to do so amid a lot of laughter and enthusiasm. The specter of Barbie's possible harm energizes the nature of the conversation, but also gives the students a truly concrete understanding of the nature of statistical variation or error. The regression equation will give a prediction for about how far Barbie will drop—but much like political polls with their plus-or-minus 5% degree of error, there is a window on either side of this estimate where Barbie could also fall. The students have to understand this concept, and also the statistical likelihood that Barbie will fall on the wrong side of this error range, and then make their case to Barbie about how long the bungee cord should be.

I've observed this activity firsthand, and the students are abuzz with energy and enthusiasm throughout the activity—which stands in stark contrast to other lectures I've seen on statistics. The amusement, especially with a tinge of the macabre, mobilizes the students' energy and efforts. This greater energy and generally positive mood, along with the challenge of the task, result in greater mobilization of resources and better, more engaged performance.

In considering how to apply affective science principles to choose classroom activities and assignments to mobilize student efforts, we'll begin by considering how to choose activities like this one that will grip our students' attention and direct it to the material at hand (*interest and curiosity*). We'll next consider how to maintain those levels of student interest and attention during the process of learning (*flow*). We'll conclude by considering whether it might be worthwhile to push students to even deeper learning by occasionally intentionally disrupting their understanding of the material (*confusion*). Since all of these affective states have in common the pursuit of knowledge or skills, we can refer to them as knowledge emotions.[2]

Interest

You are teaching a Monday morning class that serves as one of your college's general education requirements—meaning that most of the students slumped in their seats are not there because they intend on majoring in your field or because they are attracted to your course's topic. Rather, they are there because they feel conscripted. They might be undisposed toward working hard and may even be feeling a bit resentful. Beyond managing your presentation style and first impressions, your very first challenge is getting them interested. As Todd Kashdan, psychologist and author of the book *Curious?* notes, "If you want people to be interested, committed, and willing to devote effort to learning, mastering, and using these skills for the long haul, then you can't avoid the initial step of stimulating excitement" (2009, p. 188).

What determines interest? Paul Silvia, psychologist and author of *Exploring the Psychology of Interest* (2006), highlights interpretations (also called appraisals) as the key determinants of interest. He highlights two appraisals in particular: those of novelty and complexity, and of comprehensibility. Interest arises when information is new and potentially complicated, but inherently graspable. Novelty and complexity in the absence of comprehensibility only leads to confusion, which is usually not our goal. (Though, as we'll see later in this chapter, don't be too quick to dismiss the worth of confusion entirely.) Silvia canvassed a body of research on interest and found that when you manipulate topics (e.g., abstract art, poetry) to be either or both more complex or more understandable, you boost interest. Intriguingly, he also points out that interest can be "self-propelling." Interest motivates learning, which makes you more of an expert on a subject matter, but then to be interested again you have to seek out even more complex material. Interest "motivates people to learn, thereby giving them the knowledge needed to be interested" (Silvia, 2008, p. 59). Thus, it is good to lead with complex information that is nevertheless comprehensible, and then increase in complexity as the semester progresses.

Triggering interest is great, and our first step, but we can't stop there. Jerome Rotgans and Henk Schmidt (2014) point out that while many studies provide evidence on the triggers of interest, far fewer research studies tackle whether interest, once triggered, yields demonstrable changes in learning, and how to maintain interest once it has been initially triggered. Educators researching the role of interest in education have proposed two possible hypotheses for how interest relates to educational outcomes, though both are similar in that they assume that something surprising or novel is introduced into the learning environment and that this leads to learner interest. The trigger-maintenance hypothesis supposes that interest can be triggered by aspects of the situation but then also needs to be maintained for interest to remain high. This theory maps nicely onto our proposal that it is important to design classroom activities and assignments that both capture the attentional spotlight but then also hold attention long enough for students to apply their working memory to the task at hand. The second hypothesis regarding the triggers of interest concerns the fact that interest is often engaged when one realizes a gap in one's knowledge; this is appropriately called the knowledge-deprivation hypothesis. While these theories hold many similarities, one difference is that while the trigger-maintenance hypothesis assumes that interest will be maintained if the topic continues to be interesting, the knowledge-deprivation hypothesis would predict that as students work on the problem and close the gap between the knowableness of the problem and their understanding of it, interest should decrease.

Rotgans and Schmidt performed three different studies. The participants were secondary school students learning about the Japanese conquest of Singapore during the Second World War. The results weighed in on the side of the knowledge-deprivation hypothesis: interest declined as knowledge rose. Therefore it may be important to continually jump-start interest with new knowledge puzzles as students progress through a topic. Fascinatingly, one of their studies revealed that simply using the word *surprising* in the posing of the problem led to not only greater interest but also better performance on a subsequent recall task.

KNOWLEDGE EMOTIONS TEACHING PRACTICE 1: INCLUDE SELF-RELEVANT ACTIVITIES AND ASSIGNMENTS

I can almost guarantee you have had some variant of the following experience. You are in a crowded room—say, at your departmental holiday party. You are fully engaged in conversation with the interesting person in front of you, and also the bacon-wrapped scallop you are trying to subtly eat while not breaking eye contact or spilling your champagne. You are completely absorbed in these aspects of your experience and blissfully unaware of everyone else in the room and the conversations they are having. Blissfully unaware, that is, until someone across the room happens to mention your name in conversation. This instantly arrests your attention and all of a sudden you lose track of everything you were just focused on; you are now laser-focused on the source of your name, trying to hear what it is that is being said about you. This is called, as you may already know, the cocktail party effect, and it is quite reliable. We have an attentional bias toward self-relevant information, and nothing is more relevant than our own name. In fact, research done by people interested in influence and negotiation find that the more a person uses your name in conversation, the greater your liking for that person, regardless of their other attributes.

What might self-relevance look like in the classroom? Let's take an example. Benjamin Ostiguy is the associate director of operations for disability services at the University of Massachusetts–Amherst, and one of his responsibilities is to conduct training with his staff on how to interact sensitively and empathetically with students being evaluated for services. If he wanted to use a traditional educational approach, he could ask his staff to read a stiffly written article on the challenges faced by students coming in for disability assessment, then read off some PowerPoint slides with bulleted, text-based lists of information. "Students with learning disabilities may be feeling vulnerable and it is important to be sensitive," we can imagine one such bullet point reading.

Rather than taking this traditional approach, Ostiguy begins by asking his trainees to recall in detail their last health care appointment. He asks them to meditate on this last appointment and guides them through a series of detailed prompts: Why did they go? Did their doctor perform any invasive examinations? Which tests and medications were ordered and prescribed? After letting them inhabit their memories for a time, he suddenly pairs them up. He then asks them to share all of these intimate details with each other, deeply and with specifics. He reports that his students exhibit a variety of emotional responses— some laugh or smile uncomfortably, some are angry and challenge his instructions, and some freeze in fright. He lets the emotional tension build for a few minutes. Before anyone has a chance to divulge any confidential information, he breaks with the activity and reveals its true purpose: to put his trainees in the position, if but for a few moments, of what it might feel like to come into an office filled with people you may need to interact with again and reveal to them extremely personal information. Ostiguy explains that "participants have noted how the exercise helped contextualize everything that followed, and allowed them greater access to the importance of destigmatizing the process of requesting and receiving reasonable accommodations" (Ostiguy, personal communication, July 2014). His trainees not only know that the students coming into the office may be nervous and sensitive but also know what that feels like.

You may be thinking that it is easy for me, a psychologist, to prescribe self-relevance as an easy way to provoke interest and curiosity—after all, when your subject matter is the mental experiences and behaviors of human beings, everything is self-relevant. But it may be easier than you think to **make your own material self-relevant**.

James Hauri is an environmental engineer and chemistry professor at Assumption College. He has a laid-back, joke-cracking manner that puts students at ease and makes them feel comfortable sharing their thoughts in class—something he places a high premium on. At Assumption there are two separate tracks of science courses—one for the majors and one for the nonmajors. Hauri teaches a number of the nonmajor science courses and thus is taxed with making chemistry interesting to groups of students—largely freshmen who have no intention of continuing in their study of science past the bare minimum of general education requirements, and many of whom have had negative experiences in science classrooms in the past.

Hauri and I participated in an innovative, cross-paradigms teaching program at Assumption called the Tagaste Program. This program has professors from diverse fields of study link their courses together, at several points in the semester dovetailing their course content so that students see the connections between supposedly separate bodies of knowledge and appreciate the artificial nature of some of the boundaries that we enforce on knowledge. Because of this shared teaching experience, I was able to observe how Hauri engaged these nonengaged students in the subject matter—as it turns out, self-relevance was one of his go-to techniques. For instance, he had his students analyze the chemical construction of the shampoos they were using and illustrated all the unnecessary compounds that were added to them; he also reviewed how the process of cooking is essentially using heat to make chemical changes to food. In a great example of making seemingly esoteric information relatable, he published a paper with colleague Brian Niece (2013) for the *Journal of Chemical Education* detailing a lab in which students made field trips to local grocery stores to purchase samples of swordfish and tuna and then tested the level of mercury in these fish in the lab to see if they were within the range of the U.S. Food and Drug Administration's allowed limits. They situated the lesson in a dramatic discussion of the dangers of mercury in food, particularly for the medically vulnerable. With an emotional backdrop and a self-relevant exercise, students applied their effort in a much greater way than they would during a standard, rote assignment.

There are also many topics and approaches that may not be personally self-relevant, but that most students find engaging. As Kashdan notes, "When I teach my undergraduate and graduate students, I prowl for examples that intrigue them—sex, dating, drugs, violence, movies, music, and food. These examples and situations are effective because they wake students from their slumber" (2009, p. 186). While these topics may not jibe with everyone's teaching style, recall from Silvia's study that just framing problems or assignments as surprising can trigger interest. **All of our fields have unexpected discoveries or controversies or surprising relevance for daily life; find them, and build them into your courses.**

Or be creative and have students relate (and experience) the material in direct, hands-on ways. For instance, Kimberly Norris Russell of Rutgers University teaches a course in invertebrate zoology. As a major learning goal of the course is to have students master a vast array of mostly unfamiliar animal phyla (roughly thirty!), the day-in, day-out processing of the material can be a bit monotonous. To give her students a break from the drudgery of learning morphological and physiological details of the seemingly endless diversity of invertebrate groups, she has every student create a "Beast Profile" to share with the class during a brief presentation at the end of every lecture. Russell encourages students to select their focal species based on their own personal fear, disgust, or fascination:

> Having students confront their fears and/or disgust (or inspire fear or disgust in their classmates) by researching and presenting these critters to the class really seemed to make a positive impact on the overall learning environment. I don't know whether it necessarily improved their exam scores, but it certainly increased their enjoyment of the course and their appreciation of these creatures, which was one of

my goals at the outset. (Russell, personal communication, October 2015)

At the end of the semester Russell organized something she called a "Beast Feast." She and her teaching assistant cooked up all manner of tasty delicacies using invertebrates. The menu included jellyfish tentacles in sesame oil, chocolate chirp cookies (made with cricket flour), shrimp salad, shrimp cocktail, spicy crispy shrimp, steamed crayfish, Larvets Original Worm Snax (actually toasted mealworms), beer-battered clams, and grilled dried squid. The adventurous students snacked and chatted and, notes Russell,

> seemed to really appreciate the gesture, both in terms of the effort put forth and the opportunity to socialize—and study—with their peers at the event. I was impressed by how many students were willing to give everything a taste. Overall, I think it was a great way to end the semester with a positive experience, especially considering the challenging nature of the material. Invertebrate Zoology is, in fact, the Organic Chemistry of Biology and students definitely struggle! (Russell, personal communication, October 2015)

While not all of us teach subjects that allow us to literally eat our subject matter, we can all look for opportunities to liven up our own courses with self-relevance and fun activities.

Curiosity

Interest is great; it implies that we have people's attention and they are open to being moved by the information we'll provide next. But even better than triggering people into a relatively passive state of openness would be if we can get them to burn to know what comes next. As professor of psychology Ellen Winner explains, we want to induce a *rage to master* a new skill.

When you burn to know what comes next, you are feeling curious. So great is the relationship between curiosity and learning that writer William Arthur Ward calls curiosity "the wick in the candle of learning." In an investigation that nods to this quote in its title, Min Jeong Kang and her colleagues (Kang, Hsu, Krajbich, Loewenstein, McClure, Wang, and Camerer, 2009) decided to investigate just how curiosity may aid learning. They asked their college-aged participants to lie in a functional magnetic resonance imaging scanner while answering trivia questions. The participants first guessed at the answer, then rated both their confidence in their guess and how curious they were to find out the correct answer. Then they were shown the question again, this time with its correct answer. As the researchers expected, participants were most curious to find out the answers to questions that they had a middle range of confidence about answering correctly—if they were certain of the answer, curiosity was low, as it also was when they had no idea. When participants had a good hunch and wanted to confirm or disconfirm its nature, they were the most curious. This is a pattern we'll see recur in examples in the rest of this chapter. A good match between complexity/challenge and available knowledge/skills yields the best results.

In terms of brain activation, curiosity (during the guessing period) was associated with activation in regions of the brain (e.g., the caudate nucleus) known to be associated with anticipation of potential rewards. When the correct answers were revealed, the revelation that the participants' answers were incorrect was associated with the greatest activation in areas of the brain associated with learning and memory. These findings led the research team to wonder whether this association of curiosity with the anticipation of a reward and heightened activation of learning and memory regions to incorrect answers meant that curiosity had learning benefits.

To explore this possibility, Kang and her colleagues conducted a series of follow-up behavioral studies outside the fMRI scanner in which they had participants make similar trivia guesses and rate their curiosity, then return to the lab a few weeks later for a memory task. As the researchers anticipated, curiosity expressed during learning was a strong predictor of whether participants would remember the correct answer, but this effect was only true of those answers guessed incorrectly. Why only the incorrect answers? When participants guessed correctly, there was no surprise—nothing new to learn. Imagine a fox in the woods scavenging for food at the spot where she always looks first: there is no need to encode a new experience of discovering food when it's the same spot and the dozenth time. If, however, the fox finds no food there this time, or unexpectedly finds food somewhere new, *that* is important information to encode for the future. In a similar sense, one way of interpreting the data from this study is that the students made a guess, anticipated the reward of being correct (finding food), and when they found they were incorrect (no food), brain regions involved in the consolidation of memory were triggered (*Hey! Remember this next time!*).

Another group of researchers examined the curiosity-learning link by taking advantage of a newer way to examine brain data—something called functional connectivity. Essentially, different regions of our brain do not operate like individual smartphone applications working in isolation; they function interdependently, with activation spreading from one region to the next at the time that each is required for the task at hand. For instance, the task of decoding what someone is saying to you involves areas of the temporal cortex responsible for representing sound, areas involved in making sense of language, and the frontal cortex, which contributes context and past knowledge. Functional connectivity analyses essentially tell you about the degree to which the activity in certain brain regions covary over time with each other. Presumably, regions involved in related types of processing (e.g., those areas responsible for decoding sound and those for interpreting language) should demonstrate greater functional connectivity than regions that are involved in unrelated types of processing (e.g., those areas responsible for decoding shapes and those responsible for the governing of circadian rhythms).

Matthias Gruber, Bernard Gelman, and Charan Ranganath (2014) performed one of these functional connectivity studies to plumb the relationship between curiosity and learning. Like Kang and colleagues, they used an fMRI scanner while asking trivia questions; they had the subjects rate their degree of curiosity regarding the answers, and then tested their memory for these facts a day after the scan. Gruber and colleagues' results confirmed just what we might have expected: curiosity benefited learning, and its benefits could be predicted by the extent of connectivity among brain regions involved in anticipatory reward and those involved in memory consolidation. Subjects were eager to know the answers, and anticipated satisfaction from having this knowledge confirmed; these emotions were associated with better memory.

What was really intriguing about this study wasn't just that curiosity predicted better memory but also that this memory boost wasn't solely related to the answers to the questions the participants had exhibited curiosity about. The authors cleverly inserted unrelated information—pictures of random people's faces—between the curiosity-evoking questions and their answers. The result was that the participants were better able to recall faces that occurred in the interim between curiosity and learning, even though the faces had nothing to do with what they were curious about. Thus, if you choose a curiosity-invoking frame for even boring or mundane activities or lessons, you may be giving students a memory boost for all of the material that day. Thus, show a clip from an action movie that demonstrates the engineering principle you just explained, or quiz your students on some facts about your topic before presenting it, or present them with a puzzle that can only be solved if they pay attention to the lecture. Prime their curiosity pumps, and then teach them something; even if it is loosely related, they still may learn better.

KNOWLEDGE EMOTIONS TEACHING PRACTICE 2: INTRODUCE PUZZLES AND MYSTERIES

When you draw people's attention to the gap between their current state of knowledge and what they perceive as knowable, both interest and curiosity are generated. Ian Leslie's *Curious: The Desire to Know and Why Your Future Depends on It* (2014) asks us to consider the fact that prompting curiosity by highlighting knowledge gaps is the essential technique used by every storyteller—whether the story is embedded in a novel, a film, a lecture, or an advertising campaign. These narratives rely on your innate desire to find out what happens next, what the cause of the event was, and whodunit.

But these information gaps differ in the kind of curiosity they evoke and the kind of resolutions they offer. Leslie differentiates between puzzles, which open a knowledge gap that has a definite solution and a satisfying ending, and mysteries, whose solutions are much more nuanced and complex and may forever elude solving. (For instance, as Leslie hilariously asks, regarding the 1993 pop song, What *is* it that Meat Loaf won't do for love?) Police procedurals and science labs are puzzles with definite answers. They are satisfying to complete and engage interest, but—once the murderer is revealed or the lab report passed in— often quickly forgotten. Ask a *Law and Order* fan to elaborate on a recent episode, and it is likely to be a short conversation. But ask a *Lost* fan about what the ambiguous ending to the series really meant, and you better pull up a chair. Years after the finale aired, fans still speculate on the Internet about the various possibilities and the evidence that does or doesn't support their pet theories. Both puzzles and mysteries deserve a place in the classroom, and will probably serve different purposes. **Puzzles are great fodder for brief class activities or homework assignments.** Identifying a gap in knowledge and helping your students through the process of finding a meaningful solution will engender interest, and thus capture attention and motivation. This will in turn lead to satisfaction: at the end of the class period or homework assignment, your students will likely feel good that they have applied their skills to an unsolved problem and successfully resolved it. And this reward of satisfaction will further enhance motivation. So spend some time considering how you could take a topic that you might usually lecture on, and turn it into a puzzle for your students to work through on their own. In Ken Bain's excellent book *What the Best College Teachers Do*, he quotes mathematics professor Donald Sari on how he likes to teach calculus: "I want the students to feel like they have invented calculus and that only some accident of birth kept them from beating Newton to the punch" (Bain, 2011, p. 102).

While puzzles are great, **you also want to make a little room for mysteries in your classes**. Mysteries provoke a different type of curiosity than do puzzles—one called epistemic curiosity, which Leslie claims is characterized by deep, effortful, and sustained pursuit of understanding. One engages in acts of epistemic curiosity not because one wants to solve and set aside a focused question, but because the quest is its own reward, and the knowledge that the quest is ongoing is enticing. Leslie uses the example of contrasting reading a potboiler mystery with reading *The Great Gatsby*: the former offers you a packaged solution with a tidy bow; the latter can be debated and discussed endlessly, because the questions (What kind of man is Jay Gatsby? What is the true nature of the American Dream?) elude easy answers. Leslie concludes, "Mysteries are more challenging, but more sustaining. They inspire long-term curiosity by keeping us focused on what we don't know. They keep us "alive and active" even as we work in the darkness" (p. 50).

If you're reading this book, my guess is that you are an academic of some sort, and that on some level the unsolved mysteries in your field are what attracted you to it. These mysteries might have you working late into the night, or in the dawn hours before your family awakens. Mysteries have enduring motivational power.

A debate between two options or viewpoints also introduces a disequilibrium to the knowledge stream and thus should engender curiosity (D'Mello, Lehman, Pekrun, and Graesser, 2014). Students realize that there is a gap in their knowledge because there are two conflicting possibilities put forth by two individuals or groups of individuals, and they must decide which is the better one. Debates also introduce a stake to the topic: by choosing a side, students will become emotionally invested in the outcome, and this will likely encourage motivation. Or, as one Randall Munroe comic puts it, no, I'm not coming to bed, because "This is important. Someone is *wrong* on the Internet."[3]

Every field of study has its contrasting theories and explanations and frameworks. Start by giving students a solid grounding of facts so that they feel prepared to marshal arguments, then either assign them sides or have them choose one. You can make the debate as formal or informal as you wish; Google "how to structure a class debate" and you will have a wealth of options at your fingertips.

Flow

Every two years the world's attention is captured by the Olympic Games, during which we're routinely stunned by physical performances that defy the imagination. There is something inherently gripping about observing fellow human beings at the very peak of their possible performance. Seeing someone beat a previous record for speed in running, or numbers of twirls through the air on ice skates, can lead to feelings of wonder. In the 2008 games in Beijing, we collectively watched as one such human being, swimmer Michael Phelps, achieved just such a feat not once but *eight times*, taking the all-time record for the highest number of first-place finishes.

Like most Olympic athletes, Phelps admits to nothing short of relentless training. According to an interview he gave with CNN, during one phase of training he hadn't missed a day in the pool for five years. Perhaps even more remarkably, his training sessions consisted of three to six hours in the pool per day, complemented by land exercises four to five days a week. There is perhaps little mystery to *how* Phelps has become so successful, then: one achieves such near miracles through an obsessive focus on a single activity and the dedication of a truly gigantic portion of one's life to practicing it. But the real mystery to me is the *why*. Why does he do it, and what is his motivation? An Olympic medal is linked to both fame and financial rewards, but it is unlikely that this Olympic swimmer spent hour upon hour swimming as a child, thinking that the Olympics were within his grasp. Rather, Phelps reports that he found swimming to be a place of peace and focus, perhaps particularly appealing to him because he struggles with the symptoms of attention-deficit hyperactivity disorder. His mother reported that right from the beginning she could see that swimming calmed him and made him happier. Phelps reportedly has said, "I feel most at home in the water. I disappear. That's where I belong."

Phelps's experience of disappearing in the water echoes several decades of research on a mental phenomenon called flow. *Flow* is a term most associated with psychologist Mihaly Csikszentmihalyi, who elaborated on this phenomenon after he conducted extensive interviews with people with extremely high intrinsic motivation to pursue quite varied types of activities—from welding to cooking to performing surgery. He was struck that across these seemingly disparate domains and regardless of whether people pursued them for pay or for leisure (or a bit of both), people reported eerily similar clusters of experiences—namely, intense preoccupation with the activity such that the sense of self is suspended and one becomes "one with the activity"; there is a sense of disrupted time passage, and a sense of strong pleasure and reward (either during or upon completion). Athletes commonly call this experience being "in the zone."

Csikszentmihalyi studied the conditions that seem to reliably lead to the experience of flow, and it turns out that the ideal conditions are highly similar to those we just reviewed for evoking interest and curiosity, except with a focus on skill rather than knowledge. Essentially, the more closely you can match the challenge level of your activity to the very limit of your skills or abilities, the more likely it is that flow will result. When the challenge is right at this upper limit of your abilities, you have to bring to bear every bit of your resources and focus, and this intense focus seems to yield flow. If the complexity/challenge is too low, you can become bored; if it's too high, confusion, frustration, and anxiety are more likely to be elicited. While the examples above all involve physical performance (athletics, surgery) or the creation of something new (art), if the conditions are right one can experience flow even in more passive activities, such as reading. As British author Ian McEwan has stated, "Perhaps the greatest reading pleasure has an element of self-annihilation. To be so engrossed that you barely know you exist" (McEwan, 2012).

This precise match between skill and challenge may bring to developmental psychologists' minds the work of psychologist Lev Vygotsky (1980) on zones of proximal development; his focus was on children learning new tasks with the aid of parents and other educators. At certain ages, children have skills they have mastered, skills they're not yet equipped to master, and a zone in between—skills they can master only with the assistance of a parent or other guide. Vygotsky argues that parents and educators should strive to challenge children with tasks and knowledge that fall within this zone, and to be their guide in skill acquisition. Thus, not only does research on flow suggest that this optimal zone will be most motivating and enjoyable for students, but Vygotksy's theory also suggests that it may yield the best learning gains.

A second predictor of flow elicitation is clear goals and progress markers; toiling forever at some huge long-term goal for the future is not motivating and does not appear to evoke flow. Having to apply all of your effort in order to finish a painting, book chapter, or floor tiling, however, maximizes flow in the moment. Thus, clear goals and consistent feedback on progress are critical.

To investigate the role of flow in the classroom, Yi Guo, Barbara Klein, Young Ro, and Donald Rossin (2007) examined flow states and learning processes in MBA students and found that experiencing flow while learning database design predicted perceived learning, perceived skill development, and student satisfaction. Notably, greater experiences of flow did not predict objectively assessed learning as measured by scores of multiple-choice quizzes, raising the question of whether flow merely improves perceived experience rather than actual learning.

In a study with very different methods, but similar findings, Wilfried Admiraal, Jantina Huizenga, Sanne Akkerman, and Geert ten Dam (2011) explored whether using game-based learning would lead to flow and better learning in a group of high school students learning about the medieval history of Amsterdam. Students were assigned to teams and played an innovative role-playing game in which they wandered parts of Amsterdam completing assignments that involved technology (e.g., using smartphones to follow maps, watch brief videos, and take photos) and role-playing (e.g., acting out things that were experienced by people living in medieval Amsterdam). In this innovative design, students did experience flow, and greater flow was related to performance and engagement with the game. Similar to Guo and colleagues, however, Admiraal and colleagues found that flow was not related to performance on a subsequent test of how much students had learned about history.

These studies point to the idea that the elicitation of flow might lead to greater interest and motivation to learn but that, surprisingly, greater interest and motivation does not contribute to mastery of the material during test taking. Both of these studies used multiple-choice assessments of facts learned, however (the latter also included a few short essay responses—but these were scored as true or false), and it could be that greater engagement as a result of flow contributes more to longer-term or creative forms of learning, which may be difficult to detect using a multiple-choice quiz immediately following learning. It could, of course, also be that flow increases enjoyment but not greater learning. Yet if we're motivating our students and increasing their interest in the overall process of learning, this can only have good effects in the long term—even if it doesn't translate into immediate learning gains.

KNOWLEDGE EMOTIONS TEACHING PRACTICE 3:
STRUCTURE FEEDBACK TO ENHANCE COMPETENCE

By now you may be raising a skeptical eyebrow at this chapter's repeated message to match complexity to skills because, of course, we are almost never teaching individuals but instead groups of students with highly varying levels of skills and different backgrounds. It is unlikely that your classroom of thirty, sixty, or three hundred students all have the same interests and the same skills, and it may be quite difficult for you to assess these skills in a meaningful way.

But research supports that the guiding force in determining whether a person experiences curiosity with regard to a particular activity is not the existence of actual competence but instead the belief that one is competent (Kashdan and Fincham, 2004). Students may be more likely to apply the full extent of their skills (which will help them achieve flow) if they perceive themselves as being up for the challenge. Therefore, one technique you could use to bolster students' perceptions of their own competence without having to tailor activities to individual students is to **provide positive, encouraging feedback about their competence and abilities**.

When giving feedback we too often focus solely on providing information to students about what they've done wrong and areas of performance that are lacking; this is called discrepancy feedback, and it is indeed valuable and important because it highlights the gaps between students' current performance and the standard defined by the course's learning goals. This is both important not only from a pedagogical standpoint but also from an emotional one; we have seen in our discussions of flow how important it is that students have proximal goals that they can reach, and it is difficult to reach toward a goal that is undefined. Thus, we can't and shouldn't dispense with discrepancy feedback altogether, but to shore up students' sense of competency in an effort to maximize interest, curiosity, and flow, we should also be providing progress feedback, which is something that often falls to the wayside. Progress feedback is just like it sounds—**giving feedback to students about what they've done right, particularly if it is a skill that they were previously lacking**. Indeed, Lia Voerman, Fred Korthagen, Paulien Meijer, and Robert Jan Simons (2014) report that in an evaluation of seventy-eight secondary school teachers, only 6.4% of them provided progress feedback (versus 41% of them giving discrepancy feedback). I'd note that this is important not only in terms of students' feelings of competency, but also for the overall emotional tone in the classroom.

Practically, what this might look like in your own course is feedback that is both structural (embedded in your grading rubrics) and fluid from day to day (woven into how you respond to student contributions during class). In terms of grading rubrics, it might be worthwhile to consider providing both discrepancy feedback (identifying areas of needed growth) and progress feedback (intentionally highlighting what students have done well). Progress feedback can be particularly powerful if you are able to identify not only what is good in general but also where the student has gone from a discrepancy to an actualization of a given skill or piece of knowledge. For instance, you might assign a paper that is due in multiple drafts. In the first draft, you could highlight the elements of the paper that are meeting the learning goal (progress) and also the elements of the paper that are falling short of the learning goal (discrepancy). In subsequent drafts, you could identify discrepancies that have been resolved.

In terms of responding to day-to-day contributions from students in class, it is important to **look for openings for praise or validation of student contributions**. Even when a student contributes incorrect answers or opinions that reveal fundamental misunderstandings of the material, you can still highlight the logic underlying the contribution before moving on to gently correct the misunderstanding. It is easy to forget that students are in a position of low confidence in their own intellect and understanding, and that it is sometimes a huge act of bravery to volunteer for (what feels like) potential ridicule in front of a large audience of their peers. We should always reward this bravery—particularly if we want to encourage students to contribute again in the future. As a quote widely attributed to E.E. Cummings states,[4]

> We do not believe in ourselves until someone reveals that deep inside us something is valuable, worth listening to, worthy of our trust, sacred to our touch. Once we believe in ourselves *we can risk curiosity, wonder,* spontaneous delight or any experience that reveals the human spirit. (emphasis added)

It is our responsibility as practitioners of pedagogy to demonstrate to our students that we see their value, that we perceive them as worthy partners in intellectual discourse—this will open them up to be curious and achieve just the deep learning we want for them.

Finally, an easy way to create a classroom environment that is challenging and encourages pushing one's intellectual boundaries is to **practice responding to correct answers with harder questions**, something Doug Lemov (2015) calls a "stretch it" teaching technique. Asking students who give a correct answer to your question an even harder question communicates that you care deeply about their learning and that both you and they should be excited about how far you can take their knowledge. "Stretch it" questions might take the following forms: How did you come up with that answer? Why do you think that is the case? What might another possible answer be? What might be a better word, or a more precise explanation? Can you give me some evidence that backs up your answer? If I were to give you a different question, could you apply the same skills to answer it?

Finally, **pay particular attention to providing positive feedback to students who may be struggling**. In a blog post humorously titled *Why Education Needs More Radioactive Spiders* (2013), psychologist and writer Scott Barry Kaufman reviews a number of research studies suggesting that teachers tend to provide less positive feedback and poorer instructional methods (e.g., less challenging questions, discouraging head movements) to students they are aware have learning disabilities. He calls for teachers to see the untapped talent in all students, to be the "radioactive spider" (referring to the catalyst for Spiderman's abilities) that calls them forward to the challenge of developing their full potential:

> I'm convinced that there is so much more possibility in all students than we realize. Imagine what would happen if educators helped all students see in themselves what is possible, and then helped them integrate that into the core of their identity? (Kaufman 2013)

Therefore, your feedback to students—how positive it is, how much it highlights the progress they've made, and whether you simply accept their contributions or push them just a little further—can set up an environment that engenders knowledge emotions and the associated benefits to learning.

Confusion

Reading these last sections on the appraisals that lead to interest and curiosity (a precise union of complexity and comprehensibility) and the conditions that lead to the experience of flow (a perfect match between challenge and skills) may have convinced you that the road to masterful teaching always involves maneuvering our students right on the edge of comprehension, and never letting them veer into uncertainty or confusion. But is this always true? Could there be a benefit to tossing our students into a pool of knowledge before they're prepared for it, and watching them first flail, then find their inner resourcefulness and successfully master the skills needed? To answer this question we'll turn to the literature on curiosity's more ungainly sibling: confusion.

Curiosity and confusion can be considered dark mirrors of each other, in that both involve uncertainty, and both create an itch to know more. Curiosity is generally considered a positive emotion, and introduces a mystifying question that one is intrinsically motivated to answer. Confusion is generally considered a negative emotion, yet it similarly creates a mystifying situation—one in which there is motivation to puzzle one's way out. Unlike curiosity, which creates a pleasurable problem that begs to be resolved, confusion is often thought to be an aversive state that should be avoided during learning. We often do our best as instructors to avoid confusing our students; we try to be attuned to confusion's onset and provide instructional interventions to alleviate it as soon as we detect it.

But confusion may be truly fundamental to learning. For one thing, it is one of the most common emotions present during the process of learning; a meta-analysis of twenty-one experience-sampling studies revealed that it was the second most frequently cited emotion during learning (D'Mello et al., 2014). It is also an affective state that demonstrates that students are grappling with the course content in a deep way: confusion arises when a learner tries to ascertain how new information fits with his or her existing understanding of the world, finds that it doesn't fit, and adjusts knowledge structures to accommodate the new information. Adjusting one's understanding of the world to accommodate new information is, of course, one definition of learning itself. In fact, there are impasse-driven theories of learning (VanLehn, 1988) that focus on the learning power embedded in just these moments at which students reach an impasse in their understanding of the course material. These impasses require students to stop, reconsider their existing knowledge and strategies, solve a problem, and adjust their strategies—thus facilitating learning. As Sidney D'Mello, Blair Lehman, Reinhard Pekrun, and Art Graesser note, "Deep learning occurs when there is a discrepancy in the information stream and the discrepancy is identified and corrected" (2014, p. 155). Moreover, research demonstrates that confusion is actually *positively* related to learning outcomes. For instance, Scotty Craig, Arthur Graesser, Jeremiah Sullins, and Barry Gholson (2004) performed an online assessment of student emotions while learning with a tutoring system and found that confusion significantly predicted improvements in learning.

D'Mello and colleagues tested the relationship between confusion and learning in an innovative study in which their participants practiced the skill of critically evaluating research studies. They used a computer simulation in which students learned along with two animated avatars: one, called Dr. Williams, was a tutor and led the sessions; the other, called Chris, was a simulated peer who learned along with the participants. The participants, or learners, in this study were able to hold natural conversations with these computerized helpers—Dr. Williams gave information, quizzed the learner, and provided explanations for concepts. Following instruction on a concept, Dr. Williams would present Chris and the learner with a research study that was either flawed or flawless. Confusion was manipulated by having Dr. Williams and Chris sometimes agree and other times disagree. For the disagreements, the learners were invited to intervene and resolve the discrepancy. Learners were tested for knowledge of the scientific concepts before and after the session. The results indicated that learners who were confused by contradictions in the opinions of the tutor agents, or between the tutors and the truth, demonstrated superior performance on subsequent assessments of knowledge.

Confusion is a double-edged sword, of course—too much confusion and you'll disrupt learning and frustrate both your students and yourself. You want to aim for what D'Mello and colleagues call a "zone of optimal confusion." D'Mello and colleagues present the following guiding principles for implementing confusion in your classroom: (1) confusion should be appropriately and intentionally evoked in the context of a learning environment; (2) students should possess the ability to successfully resolve the confusion; and/or (3) when students cannot resolve the confusion on their own, there are appropriate scaffolds or buttresses in place to aid the students in their resolution of the confusion.

As D'Mello and colleagues conclude,

> Interventions that confuse these complacent learners via contradictions, incongruities, anomalies, system breakdowns, and difficult decisions might be just what is needed to jolt them out of their perennial state of passively receiving information and inspire them to focus attention, engage fully, think more deeply, and learn for mastery. (p. 168)

And that is a laudable goal.

KNOWLEDGE EMOTIONS TEACHING PRACTICE 4: ROUTINELY ASSESS KNOWLEDGE AND SKILL LEVELS

To successfully induce flow and also to hit the zone of optimal confusion, you need to match challenge/complexity to skill level, aiming your activities and assignments at the upper reaches of your students' skill levels (and just a bit beyond, for optimal confusion). To do this, you first have to know what your students currently know and the skills of which they are capable. Therefore, one of the most powerful practices you can use to successfully enhance flow (and the other knowledge emotions) is to **frequently and thoroughly assess what your students know**. This is partly built right into the structure of classic pedagogy. Assessments like exams and papers are, above all, meant to help both students and professors gauge which skills have been mastered and which require more work. But these assessments are typically relatively infrequent and also are designed to evaluate the degree of effort and work the students are investing in the course—in other words, to assign grades.

Better assessments of knowledge and skills would be **more frequent, low-or-no-stakes evaluations of students' mastery of knowledge**. You might start a semester with just such an assessment. For instance, I always begin my Physiological Psychology course with an anonymous pop quiz on the brain—I have students complete it individually, peer grade it, and then hand it in. The purpose of this exercise is for me to gauge where this particular batch of students stands in terms of background knowledge on the topic, because I've found it varies widely from semester to semester. This early assessment allows me to pitch the course at the optimal level right from the get-go; it has the added benefit of acting as a brief review of some of the most basic material we'll be covering for the semester *and* may enhance future learning. Research by Nate Kornell, Matthew Jensen Hays, and

Robert Bjork (2009) has demonstrated that pretesting, even when conducted in situations in which students have not previously engaged with this particular body of knowledge, predicts future memory gains, perhaps because students are anticipating where in their knowledge structures this new information will fit.

Also useful are **periodic check-ins**. One technique you may have run across is called the "one-minute paper," attributed to Frederick Mosteller (1989). The concept has evolved from a quickly written paper to take many different forms. You could use tablet devices, Blackboard quizzes, or simple index cards, but the essential component is that you ask your students at the end of each class (or segment of the course) to write about one topic or skill they feel they have mastered, and one they are still confused about. This practice allows you to detect when there are areas of concern you should address, as well as areas or topics that you have safely covered.

Among the lowest-stake assessments you can implement are questions during lecture. Lemov asks you to consider how often you have asked your classes something like the following: "OK, those are the basics of cellular structure. Everyone clear on the differences between plant and animal cells?" (2015, p. 29). Following this, you pause for all of six seconds before moving on to the next topic. Lemov points to an array of reasons why a student would not volunteer that, in fact, he or she *doesn't* know the differences between the cellular structure of plant and animal cells: from a social pressure to allow the teacher to move on, to feeling like he or she is probably the only one who doesn't understand, to general passivity, to not even realizing that it's something he or she doesn't really know. Lemov suggests a powerful teaching strategy that not only helps your students but also helps you to gauge where your class is in terms of understanding the present topic: to immediately begin replacing these "Okay, got it?" type questions with any number of better strategies that actually yield some data about how your class is doing. For instance, you could instead ask a specific question: "What does the presence of a cell wall tell me about what type of cell I'm looking at?" You could ask students to raise their hands to rate their understanding on a scale of 3 or 4. You could have them pair off into small groups to describe their understanding of the topic to each other, and then to you. The key is to **ask questions that actually reveal where your students are in their understanding of the material**.

Many professors have taken to technology to do these periodic check-ins. Your options are many: you could **use clickers**, small handheld devices allowing students to respond to polls and multiple choice questions with a quick button press, to quickly assess your students' knowledge with multiple choice questions (probably easier in science and social science than humanities). If you are intrigued by this possibility, Derek Bruff has written an entire book on the topic: *Teaching with Classroom Response Systems: Creating Active Learning Environments* (2009). You could also require students to complete quick assessments on their own time on **Blackboard or other course management websites**. Much like we discussed with pretesting, periodic testing has advantages beyond helping you maximize effort mobilization in your classes; it also yields cognitive benefits.

Knowing where your students stand in terms of knowledge and mastery of course content will benefit your teaching in all sorts of ways, but it will certainly help you pitch your content so that you are most likely to be evoking interest, curiosity, and flow, and all of their attendant learning benefits. As we just reviewed, you may occasionally want to **aim for a bit of controlled confusion**; knowing their current knowledge and skill sets will be integral for navigating your students into D'Mello's zone of "optimal confusion." And as researchers Todd Kashdan and Mantak Yuen (2007) discovered in an analysis of students across several Hong Kong schools, low levels of challenge may actually *reverse* the association between high levels of curiosity and achievement; while their observed effects are correlational, and thus we can't assume causality, students high in curiosity actually performed *worse* than their noncurious peers when they felt unchallenged. We certainly don't want to be in the position of reversing inherent curiosity and its benefits, so it is best to assess the fit between student skills and challenge often and well.

Chapter Summary

The take-home message from all of the literature we visited in this chapter is quite clear—namely, that in choosing which material to cover in your course and which assignments and activities to use in order to trigger interest, curiosity, flow, and mobilization of effort, the best thing that you can do is pay careful attention to the complexity of the material and the existing knowledge or skills of your students. The highest levels of interest (and thus engagement of attention), flow (and thus maintenance of attention and the application of working memory), and productive confusion (and thus adjustment to existing knowledge structures) will occur if you manage to navigate your students along a tight channel between the highly complex and the challenging. Aim for within their capabilities, only once in a while letting them veer off course into something more complex than their current capabilities allow in order to challenge their existing knowledge structures and engage in deep learning. If in chapter 3 we concluded that you are the weather of the classroom, determining the conditions of the sail, here we must conclude that you are also the navigator.

Further Reading

Curious about curiosity? I have two book suggestions for you, both written for the popular public: see Leslie, Ian. 2014. *Curious: The desire to know and why your future depends on it*. New York: Basic Books; and Kashdan, Todd. 2009. *Curious? Discover the missing ingredient to a fulfilling life*. New York: Harper Collins.

Intrigued by the **real-time tracking of emotions during the process of learning**? See Calvo, Rafael A., D'Mello, Sidney, Gratch, Jonathan, and Kappas, Arvid. 2014. *The Oxford handbook of affective computing*. New York: Oxford University Press.

Want to know **more about flow**? See Csikszentmihalyi, Mihaly. 1990. *Flow: The psychology of optimal experience*. New York: HarperCollins.

Are you planning a new course for the first time, and feeling a little lost as to how to begin selecting assignments and activities in order to **be sure your teaching activities and assessments are integrated with your learning goals**, as well as meeting the requirements of skill and challenge I've been discussing in this chapter? See Fink, L. Dee. 2013. *Creating significant learning experiences: An integrated approach to designing college courses*. San Francisco: Jossey-Bass.

NOTES

1. This activity is listed across multiple K–12 education sites.
2. Again, whether affective phenomena like curiosity and flow are emotions or whether they are instead motivational states or complex blends of cognition, motivation, and behavioral tendencies

is a question bigger than this book. For some reflections on this issue, see chapter 1.

3. Randall Munroe, "Duty Calls," https://xkcd.com/386/.

4. While widely attributed to the poet, these words do not appear in his poems or his one prose work. Some scholars have speculated that it might have appeared in his letters. It is also possible that this quote has been misattributed.

5

FUELING THE FIRE

Prolonging Student Persistence

Catherine Caldwell-Harris is a cognitive psychologist at Boston University. When I was an undergraduate, I enrolled in her introductory developmental psychology course. She was younger than most of the other faculty members with whom I had taken courses, and her energy was infectious and almost dizzying. The class watched with wide eyes as Caldwell-Harris paced the stage of the large amphitheater, extolling the virtues of self-directed learning and passionately railing against doing work for work's sake. She noted that rather than specific assignments, we would have to craft our own work, informed by our personal interests and in a form that we would enjoy working in. These three projects would become our "portfolio," which would be graded at the end of the semester. As I was one of those stick-in-the-mud students who just wanted to know how to do everything the professor wanted so that I could collect my A, I found the idea of doing three . . . *somethings* . . . on any topic I wanted to be worryingly amorphous. I fretted for a while, but then got to work.

I honestly don't recall what two of my projects were, but the third lit a fire of deep interest in me. I decided to participate in one of the ad hoc poster presentation sessions Caldwell-Harris had set up, and presented a cross-cultural inventory of different methods of parental discipline. I found surprisingly little research that considered many cultures at once, and so was driven deep into the anthropology stacks at the BU library, blowing dust off musty primary source accounts of times lived among various isolated cultures. I spent many late nights poring over these accounts, astounded by the diversity in human behavior. This was one of the highlights of my undergraduate career, and the best representation of my idealized portraits of what academia would be when I was an adolescent looking forward to college. Caldwell-Harris had created an assignment for which I had high perceptions of both *control* (I could study almost any topic, in whatever format I wanted) and *value* (I could choose topics that I found inherently valuable and interesting). The result was profound learning. The experience and the content has stayed with me for over fifteen years since.

This type of experience is the holy grail of teaching, what we want for our students to experience in all of our courses—engaged, self-directed learning that results in a shift in how they see the world, and something that lasts for their lifetimes. How can we harness the principles of affective science to craft experiences like these for our students? In chapter 4 we considered how to choose activities and assignments that enliven student interest and curiosity to get them working—how to mobilize their efforts. In this chapter we'll consider how to choose activities and assignments that engender longer-term focus and motivation and reduce procrastination—how to prolong their persistence.[1]

Control-Value Theory

For the last several decades, Reinhard Pekrun of the University of Munich has studied students' emotions during the process of learning and their relation to motivation, examining this question from almost every perspective possible, from having students recall past experiences, to querying students about classes just completed, to having students track their emotions during tests and other classroom activities in real time. As Pekrun, Thomas Goetz, Wolfram Titz, and Raymond Perry conclude, "There was virtually no major human emotion not reported by our participants, disgust being the only notable exception" (2002, p. 93). Anxiety was the most frequently mentioned emotion, representing about 15–25% of these reports. While it is perhaps no surprise that students are anxious during test taking and group presentations, anxiety was even present for low-performance activities like studying at home.

Pekrun and his colleagues organize these achievement emotions and their relation to motivation along two dimensions: positivity/negativity (often called valence) and activation/deactivation (often called arousal). For instance, along the activation dimension, positive activating emotions include enjoyment of learning, pride, and hope for future success, whereas negative activating emotions include frustration, anxiety, and guilt/shame. Along the deactivation dimension, positive deactivating emotions include satisfaction, relief, and contentment, whereas negative deactivating emotions include boredom and lack of hope. Not surprisingly, positive activating emotions are found to be linked to motivation, and negative deactivating emotions to a lack of motivation.

Positive deactivating emotions and negative activating emotions relate to motivation in a more complex fashion. Positive deactivating emotions such as satisfaction may reduce motivation in the moment, but because they involve positive reinforcement may increase motivation in the longer term. Negative activating emotions can reduce motivation (e.g., fear leading to freezing), but at lower levels could fuel motivation (e.g., worry leading to hard work to prevent a poor outcome). In addition to varying according to valence and activation, emotions in the classroom also vary in terms of the object or cause of the emotion and whether this cause is related to the past, present, or future. For instance, a student concerned about a graded assessment could be feeling emotional in a way that is anticipatory (hope that he or she will do well on an assessment, fear that that will not be the outcome) or retrospective (pride at having performed well, shame or anger at having received a poor grade).

These emotions during learning relate significantly to students' academic achievement across numerous ways of measuring both the emotions and the achievement. As Pekrun and colleagues note,

> Moving beyond cross-sectional correlations, university students' emotions measured early in the semester predict cumulative grades as well as final course exam scores at the end of the semester. With the exception of relief, positive emotions such as academic enjoyment, hope, and pride predicted high achievement, and negative emotions predicted low achievement. (2002, p. 99)

Corresponding to the complicated nature of activating negative emotions (does anxiety help or hurt?), negative deactivating emotions like hopelessness and boredom had more of a dampening effect on achievement than did activating negative emotions like anxiety or shame.

But Pekrun wasn't satisfied with simply cataloging these relationships; he wanted to understand the mechanisms or the underlying processes by which emotions in academic work predict student success (and lack of success) so well. This later work led him to propose an organizing framework through which to understand research on emotions in the classroom. He calls this theory the control-value theory (Pekrun, Frenzel, Perry, and Goetz, 2007), and in developing it, he focuses on appraisals as critical predictors of which emotions might arise in the process of an academic experience.

Appraisals refer to a person's evaluation or interpretation of a situation or emotional stimulus, and they are vital contributors to the emotional response. Every time something is introduced or changed in your environment, you mentally (and often automatically, without conscious control) evaluate whether the change is positive or negative, under your control or someone else's, relevant to your goals or not, and so on. For instance, if you are in an airport security line and out of the corner of your eye you detect someone running, this is likely to grab your attention. You might turn to get more information, see a running child just ahead of a running adult and appraise the situation as benign and irrelevant to you—your emotional response mutes, and you turn away and reattend to the task of getting through the line. If, however, you turn and a large man is running toward you with a dangerous weapon in his hand, your appraisal of the situation and emotional response will be quite different.

Two types of appraisals are critical for Pekrun's control-value theory. The first appraisal is that of control: to what degree students feel in control of the activities and outcomes that are important to them. The second appraisal is that of value—to what degree the activity or material represents meaning or worth to students. Pekrun argues that appraisals of high control and high value will both independently and synergistically contribute to which emotions students experience and how those emotions contribute to motivation and learning. For example, if students perceive their control to be low—either perceiving that they could work very hard and never get a good grade, or perceiving that the class is an "easy A" and it doesn't matter if they apply effort or not—they are unlikely to experience positive activating emotions, and this will not fuel motivation or learning success.

In terms of value, if students perceive the assigned subject matter as having no relevance for either their daily life or their eventual career, positive activating emotions are also likely to be infrequent even if control is high. Having read the previous chapters of this book, it will not surprise you to learn that Pekrun also sees strong roles for cognitive resources (such as attention and memory) and motivational processes in both feeding into and being influenced by these control and value appraisals. That is, experiencing high control and value will result in positive emotions, which will influence variables like motivation, levels of attention, extent of memory processing, and self-regulation of behavior. These effects will then lead to greater success in the classroom, which will result in even greater achievement emotions and also greater levels of control and value. Similarly, one can imagine a certain circularity in which negative emotions in the classroom lead to poorer performance, detrimentally impacting control and value appraisals, which thus lead to lower motivation and even more poor performance.

Moreover, Pekrun points out that appraisals are most important early on in a learning experience (e.g., the first few days of your Anatomy and Physiology class). Students who have had several positive experiences in a given classroom then anticipate future enjoyment without the need for effortful appraisals of control or value—they come into the classroom with a habitualized appraisal or anticipated enjoyment—and vice versa for a classroom in which they've experienced low levels of control and value. This echoes our consideration in chapter 3 of how important the first few classes are.

In a direct test of the idea that control over learning activities yields benefits, Erika Patall, Harris Cooper, and Susan Wynn (2010) worked with high school teachers to randomly assign students to either have or not have a choice in which homework assignments they completed. While choice did not impact all aspects of learning (e.g., negative emotions during completion or about how valuable they thought the homework was), students reported more interest, enjoyment, and competence during completion of the choice homework than the nonchoice and scored higher on the subsequent unit test. The researchers also observed a trend whereby students tended to complete more of the homework when it was of their choosing. Given that the choice employed was pretty limited—students were choosing between two very similar homework assignments, and thus their influence was pretty nominal—these are compelling effects.

What about value? In a direct test of manipulating appraisals, Chris Hulleman, Olga Godes, Bryan Hendricks, and Judith Harackiewicz (2010) asked students in introductory math and psychology classes to free-write on the topic of how the material they were learning either did or did not apply to their daily lives. They found that writing about the perceived usefulness of the material yielded benefits in reported interest, especially for those who were identified as potentially struggling with the material.

Prolonging Persistence Teaching Practice 1: Give Control, Maximize Value

Given the literature we've just reviewed, maximizing students' sense of control and value over their work should yield ample benefits to their learning. Luckily, there are several routes we can take to influence student appraisals of control and value.

The most straightforward route to maximizing students' sense of control is quite simply to **give them control** by giving them choices in activities and assignments wherever possible. In addition to the gains of greater completion, interest, enjoyment, and perceived competence, **building choices into your syllabus** may have other benefits. For instance, if rather than assigning the entire class the same literature review paper topic you give students a choice of topic (within a given domain) and a choice of format (e.g., literature review paper or class presentation), they are likely to choose activities for which they have the requisite skills. Having the skills to meet the challenge, they will be more likely to experience flow and all of its attendant benefits. It may also mix up the type of assignments you are grading a bit, which is never a bad thing. Grading ten papers, ten oral presentations, and ten poster presentations on thirty different aspects of a topic sounds a great deal more interesting to me than grading thirty term papers on the same exact topic.

You can also **allow for choice on in-class assessments**. This can be as simple as offering three essay questions and allowing the students to choose which two to answer. Such a practice is likely to reduce test anxiety as well as amplify appraisals of control and mastery; it may also have an unexpected benefit for you in terms of reducing the dreaded postexam "grade grubbing." If a student is trying to argue that your exam question was obscurely worded or otherwise ambiguous, you can point to the fact that they could have chosen a different question to answer.

Fundamentally, giving students control over the nature of their assignments (or at least the perception of control) will also increase appraisals of value, as students are most likely to choose activities that they find naturally rewarding or interesting. So **the first way to maximize value is to back up one step and maximize control**.

Beyond choice, what other ways do we have of maximizing perceived value? In a review of motivational interventions in the classroom, Chris Hulleman and Kenneth Barron (2015) highlight five different possible routes to value: **(1) choosing fun and enjoyable activities that maximize interest and thus intrinsic value; (2) appealing to self-relevance; (3) highlighting the relevance for current or future goals; (4) highlighting the importance of pleasing others; and/or (5) offering rewards or threatening punishments.** The first of these (emphasizing interest) we discussed in chapter 4 regarding mobilizing student efforts through maximizing interest, curiosity, and flow. The last of these (rewards and punishments) is already embedded into the design of higher education: grades, the dean's list, academic probation.

Utility. In terms of Hulleman and Barron's second suggestion, you can enhance a sense of value by **tailoring the focus of class activities such that they have utilitarian relevance to students' daily lives.** This is a bit like self-relevance, as mentioned in chapter 4, but with an added focus on the outcome or the skill to be mastered. For instance, when teaching statistics in psychology, many textbooks and professors choose examples from areas of psychology known to be of high interest or value to students so that those students can see that the mathematical concepts are not purely theoretical but can also yield answers to important questions for therapists (Which clinical approach resulted in significantly lower depression?) or child psychologists (What are the predictors of good success in an early intervention program?).

In a blog post titled "Managing up When You're on the Bottom," freelance writer and editor Steve DeMaio discusses an experience he had while teaching English as a second language (ESL) to recently immigrated students in Cambridge, Massachusetts. DeMaio had been reading articles on the topic of "managing up," which refers to techniques one can use to affect the behavior of people in authority over you in the workplace. It occurred to him that these articles were always pitched at upwardly mobile, career-focused people who were likely working under similarly management-focused superiors. But really, he reasons, the people who would most benefit from such techniques are people who work with little autonomy and people who are unskilled in management.

DeMaio brought up this issue with his ESL students and asked their opinion. They immediately began to share stories about what it was like to work in positions of little power, with few options to influence the actions of their higher-ups. A student he calls Lydia related a story in which she was verbally reprimanded by her boss. She was quite aware of multiple dynamics influencing both her boss's negative mood and the general confusion in the laboratory where they worked—and in fact she was reprimanded because she was away from her post trying to solve some of these problems—but given her rudimentary language skills she had a difficult time quickly and concisely expressing herself.

DeMaio used this opportunity to have his students brainstorm and then practice phrases that would be helpful in similar circumstances should they occur in the future—phrases like "May we sit down to discuss this?" or "Please give me the chance to explain." He also conducted a discussion activity—in English—on the topic of "managing up," which he reports his students found both apt and humorous. This useful activity and discussion had clear value to the students. They may well have found themselves implementing some of the phrases practiced and thus hopefully improving their experience at their jobs. Given the evidence in the literature we have reviewed on value appraisals, this activity likely far more effectively increased DeMaio's students' facility with the English language than just flipping to the next canned lesson in his textbook would have done.

Transcendent purpose. When it isn't obvious or easy to tailor the actual activity or assignment to amplify a student's sense of value, one can always take the route of **explicitly calling out the value in terms of manipulating purpose appraisals**, a tactic echoed by Hulleman and Barron's third and fourth suggestions of highlighting goal relevance or importance for others. Acknowledging that a given activity or practice can be onerous but making transparent the purpose of such a practice for course-related goals ("Yes, studying research methods is about as boring as you get, but once we master these skills we'll be able to critically evaluate cutting-edge research on this topic") or more transcendent purposes ("Knowing something about climate science will help me make informed judgments about my energy use and which politicians to support") can yield benefits in perceived value and thus motivation and performance.

A powerful example of including transcendent purpose in your courses is to **implement a service learning component**. Service learning combines community service and pedagogy in a way that enriches both; courses that implement service learning include as part of the course requirements a certain number of hours of community service, but ideally the type of service that complements the learning goals of the course. For instance, accounting students might volunteer to help elderly people in the community with tax preparation, education students might volunteer to tutor refugee children integrating into the public school systems, or computer science students might help local non-profits develop new websites for their organizations. Mike Land, adept director of my college's Community Service Learning program, reflects on moments of pure connection—and even love—while engaging in service:

> They lift us out of our immediate context, remind us of vaster worlds and alternate realities—ones that could just as easily be true, if we simply choose to act that way, and apply some imagination to how our routines can expand to acknowledge our now broader sense of possibilities. (2013)

These are learning opportunities that allow our students to hone their practical skills, give back to the world in a meaningful way, *and* broaden the horizons of what seems possible to them. What more could we ask?

Role-playing. Finally, when both of these techniques have failed or aren't applicable, one can always **use a role-playing technique to artificially boost perceived value**. An amusing and fascinating example of this outside higher education is the German government using a role-playing exercise to train new diplomats. They call it Projekt Exodus, and it will reportedly involve trainees living on a retired destroyer ship, acting out scenarios from the popular science fiction drama *Battlestar Galactica*, in which the world is taken over by robotic usurpers. Rather than sticking its diplomats in a hotel ballroom to view Power-Point slides on how to best respond in an emergency, the German government has opted to immerse these diplomats in an emotional, seemingly high-stakes scenario that they will have to work together to resolve. One can imagine that such a training exercise will yield more focus, engagement, and persistence in effort than would the hotel ballroom scenario.

If you are teaching in history or another field that involves revisiting complex events that unfold over time, you might consider Mark Carnes's acclaimed Reacting to the Past model. This technique, described at length in his book *Minds on Fire* (2014), casts students in the roles of major players in historic events. On their own time, students read and investigate relevant texts and accounts of the events. In class, often for a month or longer, students play out major debates and decisions. In an article for the *Chronicle of Higher Education* on the topic (2011), Carnes reports that students engaged in Reacting to the Past often go well beyond the class requirements to fulfill their roles, staying up late to read primary source documents, debating issues back in the dorms, and so on.

In a course on Western civilization led by professor of history Paul Fessler, students playing a game set during the French

Revolution were so alarmed by the news that they might run out of time to finish the game that they volunteered to come to class a half hour early for the remainder of the semester—even though the class started at 8 A.M. As Carnes reports,

> "Every student felt a strong personal investment in their roles," . . . explained Nate Gibson, a student in the class. "We read more in the weeks of the game than we had at any time before in the class. We plowed through the game manual, our history texts, Rousseau, you name it. We spent hours writing articles. I spent several all-nighters editing my faction's newspapers, and other editors did too. It had become more than a class to us by that point. The early-morning sessions were the only way to honor the sacrifices that everybody had made." (2011)

There are probably many reasons why Reacting to the Past is so effective in motivating students, including the competitive spirit it engenders and the fact that it taps into social, team-based motivations. But I highlight it here because it also is a good example of introducing value to class activities. No longer are historical events facts to be memorized or readings to be passively slogged through; rather, they are suddenly vital tools for the winning of a game. The process also transforms a previously inert litany of pieces of information into a story with real characters that you meet and speak with—and we have already discussed the privileged nature of stories in engendering curiosity and enhancing memory (see chapter 4). If Reacting to the Past sounds intriguing to you, in addition to Carnes's book, there is an annual conference at Barnard College and many resources online, including many already filled-out worksheets and other materials.

While you probably don't have access to a retired German destroyer and may not want to spend a good chunk of an entire semester re-creating a historical or fictional drama, smaller-scale role-playing exercises may maximize value in situations where it is difficult to naturally engender interest. In fact, we've already seen two examples of such role-playing in chapter 4: the students pretending to advise Barbie in her bungee-jumping endeavors and the disability office employees pretending to be at a medical appointment. Considering whether you can make a story or game out of an activity may be a way to hack value into an activity that is otherwise lacking in it.

Self-Regulation

In the previous section we framed appraisals as being inherent to the activities that we are choosing for our students: we are the directors of the interpretations or relevance, and the appraisals are embedded in the activities or assignments. However, our students are autonomous beings who are engaging in their own, personalized appraisal processes pretty much continuously, and who are also regulating their own choices and behaviors. As such, let's consider how we may intervene in their appraisals.

You have likely had the experience of being solicited by a friend to sponsor him or her to run, swim, or walk for a charity. Some of these requests probably come from fitness junkies who figure they might as well do some good while they're running their third marathon of the year. But for every solicitation from your personal Olympian in training, there is one from a former couch potato who downloaded an app and pursued a running program just for this event. If you were to ask him or her about the motivation for signing up for such an out-of-character task, I bet you'd find that it is a combination of wanting to get fit and wanting to give back and help others. If you probed further, you'd likely find that this person decided to combine these activities because the goal of helping people aids the goal of getting fit; it keeps him or her working on fitness past the point he or she might otherwise; it prolongs persistence.

Let's take a new runner. It can be hard to wake up earlier than usual, dislodge the cat nestled on your legs, and lace up, morning after morning. The amorphous goal of "getting fitter and being healthier" can seem pretty distant and intangible when squinting in the predawn light, shivering in the cold, and contemplating forcing your body through the strenuous movements involved in running. For many of us, "getting fit" isn't terribly emotional; it is something we know we should do, but it is hard, and it requires repeated effort, and with slow progress. On the other hand, the thought of saving a child from cancer or kidney disease is a much more vivid and compelling motivation; so too is the imagined praise and good wishes of your social others when you successfully run the race, or (on the flip side) the flush of imagined embarrassment and shame should you back out and have to admit it to your sponsors. These anticipated emotions can make it easier to yank yourself from your bed and out into the chill.

Regulating one's experiences and behavior to bring it in line with larger goals is called self-regulation, and it is the object of great study in motivation science. If you're the new runner, it is almost like you are two selves: you are the childlike, hedonism-craving self who really, really wants to stay bundled under the duvet; you are also the adult, officious self who applies logic and reason and the application of goal setting to get out of bed and onto the streets. You somewhat laboriously bring to bear other appraisals (this run is critical for raising money for a sick child) and remind yourself of potential future emotions (pleasure at socially perceived success, shame at socially perceived failure) in order to find the motivation to get out of bed.

How important is self-regulation to success? In one of the most famous experiments in psychology, Walter Mischel of Stanford University asked a group of toddlers to sit down in front of a marshmallow . . . and not eat it. Specifically, he told them they could eat it if they really wanted to, but if they could manage to sit alone with the marshmallow and refrain from eating it for a set period of time, they would be rewarded with *two* marshmallows to eat. Mischel and his collaborators ran a number of studies similar to this, and in some of the most remarkable ones, they followed these toddlers over decades, and found that those who could delay gratification later in life had an array of more positive life outcomes, such as lower body mass index (Schlam, Wilson, Shoda, Mischel, and Ayduk, 2013) and higher SAT scores (Shoda, Mischel, and Peake, 1990). Though some people have raised questions about the methodology in these studies, others have replicated the basic finding that better self-regulation predicts better performance and achievement across a wide range of domains.

Self-regulation has obvious relevance to student success in the classroom, from the benefits of turning down an array of tempting activities in favor of attending class to turning attention away from the smartphone and toward the class discussion. How can we assist them in doing so? The best approach may be to give them a hand in taking their initial appraisals of control and value and helping them to *reappraise*.

Reappraisals

We've so far been discussing ways of making course material inherently of high control and value to students. But sometimes, the material or skill to be mastered is intrinsically uninteresting to many. Conjugating foreign verbs, basic math drills, identifying independent and dependent variables in research designs: these are necessary elements of learning that don't exactly energize scores of students. What can we do when it is tremendously difficult to find a way to naturally evoke emotions to engender motivation?

One of the most active areas of self-regulation research is the study of what is called cognitive reappraisal, which refers to the reconstrual of the original appraisal of an event or thought in order to alter its emotional impact. In one classic experiment of reappraisal, James Gross (1998) asked participants to watch an extremely graphic video of an actual (i.e., not simulated) amputation. Some of the participants were instructed to watch the video as they would normally watch any video. Some of the participants were instructed merely to control their facial expressions during the viewing—to mask the emotions they were feeling behind a neutral face. Finally, the critical third group was instructed to reappraise the video—specifically, by taking the perspective of a doctor or other medical professional, viewing the video from the objective, clinical viewpoint that such a perspective would require ("Ah, now they are sterilizing the site to prevent infection"). The reappraisal group reported the lowest levels of disgust toward the video, and exhibited less physiological reactivity than the people instructed to suppress their emotional expressions.

Decades of research have demonstrated that cognitive reappraisal is an effective strategy for reducing emotional arousal and that regular use of reappraisal is linked to lower levels of depression and anxiety and higher levels of positive emotions and well-being (Gross, 2013a). If we want students to reduce deactivating emotions in the classroom and increase activating emotions, supporting their reappraisals may be an effective target for intervention.

Can we help students reappraise inherently dull class activities as important and interesting? David Yeager and colleagues (Yeager, Henderson, Paunesku, Walton, D'Mello, Spitzer, and Duckworth, 2014) discuss "purpose in learning," a term that encompasses motivation to learn both for self-related reasons (e.g., earning a degree, applying skills) and self-transcendent reasons (e.g., improving the world or the welfare of others). Purpose in learning can spur motivation—especially in cases where a task is tedious or otherwise onerous. As an example of such onerous tasks, Yeager and colleagues note that in a representative survey, roughly half of middle school students polled claimed they would rather take out the trash or eat broccoli than do math homework.

In four studies, these authors demonstrated that asking high school and college students to ponder the transcendent purposes their learning might have and how it might one day connect with bettering the world improved subsequent performance not only on single examinations but also overall grade point average (GPA) in math and science-related courses. Compellingly, they also explored the *how* of these effects. In one study, they exposed high school students to the idea that practicing math skills could help prepare them for their future careers, and then had them complete a task in which they could allocate their time to solving boring math problems or to consuming tempting media (watching short viral videos selected to be entertaining or playing Tetris). Those participants who reported greater self-transcendent purpose in learning solved more of the math problems, despite rating them as just as boring as those with lower purpose in learning. In a follow-up study conducted on college students taking a psychology class, inducing a self-transcendent purpose resulted in participants spending approximately twice as much time on review problems for an exam than a group that didn't receive the purpose induction. Yeager and colleagues conclude, "All told, it seems that when adolescents had a personally important and self-transcendent 'why' for learning they were able to bear even a tedious and unpleasant 'how'" (2014, p. 574).

In an explicit examination of whether supporting reappraisals could impact positive emotions and effective learning, Amber Chauncey Strain and Sidney D'Mello (2014) asked participants to study the U.S. Constitution and the Bill of Rights. They reasoned that this subject matter is one that is common to most schools in the United States and is often perceived as low in value/utility. Following Gross's tradition from the amputation study, they asked participants to take on an expert perspective—in this case, of someone applying for a job in a law firm. They reasoned that this would increase the perceived value of the information to be learned. The results revealed that those participants who took the perspective of the job applicant reported greater degrees of positive involvement in the task, less confusion and frustration, and improved learning on some (though not all) of the measures. Put another way, manipulating appraisals resulted in more positive experiences and better learning.

In sum, either increasing students' sense of control and value in their coursework, evoking a more transcendent purpose (as in Yeager and colleagues calling students' attention to the fact that better math skills for a populace might yield a better world in which to live), or designing creative ways to artificially evoke purpose (as in Strain and D'Mello asking students to role-play someone who needs the relevant information or skills for a job interview), may maximize the kinds of long-term motivation required for longer assignments.

Attributional Retraining

These suggestions for maximizing control suggest that, as instructors, we're the ones in charge of whether or not students perceive themselves as being in control. However, extensive evidence indicates that a sense of control in academic learning isn't just a state variable but also a trait variable. State variables are in the moment and change from activity to activity, whereas trait variables are those that are specific to the individual and show less variation from circumstance to circumstance.

To a large degree, as instructors we can manipulate the state variables (the circumstances of the activity or assignment) and I have just discussed how to structure your class so as to amplify state control. It is a great deal more difficult to manipulate the traits of our students, but it is also important to do so, because not only might higher control impact their learning in a direct sense (yielding benefits in motivation and positive activating emotions) but research shows that students low in perceived control often benefit less from various other classroom improvements (e.g., increased teacher enthusiasm) than those high in perceived control (Haynes, Perry, Stupnisky, and Daniels, 2009). Levels of perceived control appear to be a highly important predictor of good outcomes in the classroom, such as low levels of boredom and anxiety, better self-monitoring, and better grades (Haynes et al., 2009), and thus we should work hard to amplify perceived control.

Thankfully, while it is difficult to change stable, trait-like characteristics, research on attributional retraining in the classroom indicates that it is not impossible to do so. Attributional retraining is an intervention technique that directly targets students' appraisals of their own learning—specifically, one type of appraisal that is called an attribution. Attributions are the appraisals we make about cause and effect, success and failure: Why wasn't I invited for an interview? What was the bomber's motive? Why did I receive a C minus on this exam? Studies in the classroom have focused on the attributions students make about their academic successes and failures. In a review of the literature on attributions in the classroom, Sandra Graham and April Taylor (2014) note that when students are attributing causes for success and failure, these tend to take focus on ability (both innate and acquired through practice), effort, difficulty of the assignment, luck, mood, and help or interference from others. Of course, most of us would prefer to attribute our successes to our ability and effort and our failures to bad luck or others' interference—a tendency that has been labeled hedonic bias. But if you attribute the cause of your poor exam grade to bad luck or the teacher being out to get you, that isn't going to put you in good stead to prepare better for the next exam. And if you are a student who routinely makes these unstable, external sorts of attributions, it can have a detrimental effect on your progress in the long term.

Enter attributional retraining, which encourages students to attribute both their successes and their failures to factors they can control (e.g., degree of effort or quality of study strategies) rather than uncontrollable factors (e.g., bad luck, poor teaching, an overly difficult or easy test; Perry, Stupnisky, Hall, Chipperfield, and Weiner, 2010). The form of attributional retraining varies from researcher to researcher; among other techniques, people have used instructional videos, self-reflective writing assignments, and group discussions, all centered around encouraging students to own both their successes and failures. Decades of work on the topic have suggested that attributional retraining is associated with nearly every good outcome one can think of, from improved student ratings of how much they've learned to greater enjoyment of academic work to higher grades (often on the order of a letter grade or two; Haynes et al., 2009).

For example, in an investigation aimed at disentangling the cognitive and emotional effects of attributional retraining, Nathan Hall and colleagues recruited over seven hundred undergraduates taking an introductory psychology course (Hall, Perry, Goetz, Ruthig, Stupnisky, and Newall, 2007). In the two retraining conditions, they gave all of the students a handout that detailed the many positive effects of attributing failures to effort rather than ability and included suggestions for how one might change one's attributions. They then asked the students to complete a writing assignment elaborating on these attributions: half were asked to emphasize the cognitive elements, and the other half were asked to emphasize the emotional elements. The cognitive group summarized the handout, and then wrote about how it might apply to some case studies of student failures. The emotional group wrote about recent failures of their own and possible causes. The researchers anticipated that students who do or do not routinely use a style of cognition called elaborative thinking might respond differentially to these interventions. Elaborative thinkers were likely to relate course content to other material from classes or daily lives, think up their own examples, and so on. In a control condition, students completed the questionnaire measuring elaborative thinking but did not participate in any retraining.

As Hall and colleagues had anticipated, all students benefited from attributional retraining compared to the control students, but their benefits differed based on the types of thinking they regularly employed. Students who regularly engaged in elaborative thinking and studying benefited most from cognitive retraining, whereas students low in elaborative thinking benefited *only* from the emotional retraining. Since elaborative studying is linked with good educational outcomes in its own right, students low in elaborative thinking are probably the most in need of intervention, and it seems that they may benefit most if asked to think about how the material might apply to their own lives. Notably, mediation analyses suggested that the benefit that high elaborators experienced was explained by changing expectations regarding future behavior, whereas the benefit the low elaborators experienced was explained by increased positive emotion.

In another direct test of attributional retraining, Raymond Perry, Robert Stupnisky, Nathan Hall, Judith Chipperfield, and Bernard Weiner (2010) assessed 457 first-year students following their first test and then subsequently over two semesters. Participants in the attributional retraining group completed a one-hour training session. First, they elaborated on their own explanations for their recent test grade. Next, they watched a ten-minute video explaining adaptive versus maladaptive attributions and how shifting attributions could benefit future performance. Finally, they completed some exercises meant to drive home the main points of the video.

While students who were already high in performance as indicated by the first test did not seem to benefit much from attributional training, the students with low to average performance had better test grades, final grades, and first-year GPAs when compared to the group not retrained. Notably, several of these outcomes were a full letter grade's improvement, were measured a full semester after the retraining, and encompassed a variety of subjects and modes of testing. Even more encouraging, a posttest months after the initial attributional retraining revealed that students in the treatment condition had shifted their explanations of failure specifically toward study strategies and away from poor professor quality. As Perry and colleagues emphasize, the length of time after initial training and the de-emphasis on the role of instructor quality in particular holds promise for students carrying these attributions into future learning environments.

Mind-Sets

If you have spent any time reading current pedagogical literature (or have checked out the books on Bill Gates's 2015 reading list), you may have read the previous section on attributional retraining and thought of Carol Dweck's (2006) work on mind-sets. Mind-set theory is more focused than appraisal theory in that it centers specifically on issues of learning, talent, and performance, but is more broad than attributional retraining, as the latter targets the narrower topic of reasoning about success and failure.

In essence, mind-set theory focuses on whether you see intellectual and skill-based aptitudes as static, immovable, and determined by powerful forces like genes and upbringing (called a fixed mind-set) or instead as fluid, dynamic, and determined by the effort and practice you apply (called a growth mind-set). In a fixed mind-set, struggles and failures are seen as inevitable confirmation of lack of talent: "I'm just not a math person." In a growth mind-set, struggles and failures are seen as opportunities for learning and increasing of skill: "I performed poorly in that race, but now I know what to do for next time." Even if you are new to mind-sets, you can probably guess that it is the latter mind-set that is associated with all sorts of surprisingly powerful positive outcomes in terms of performance. Give people the sense that they are the masters of their own aptitude and they will flourish.

The interventions for mind-sets are quite similar to those of attributional retraining: worksheets priming the idea of growth mind-sets, video trainings, workshops, and the like. For instance, research scientist Lisa Sorich Blackwell received a generous grant from the U.S. Department of Education's Institute of Education Sciences to develop

> research-based interactive Professional Development Modules and Webinars that teach educators how the brain learns, how a growth mindset promotes student motivation and achievement, and how to support this mindset in their students; an online Growth Mindset Toolkit with resources for teachers and students to use in the classroom; and an online professional learning community where educators can share questions, experiences, ideas, tools and strategies with colleagues and experts in the field. (Blackwell, n.d.)

David Paunesku and colleagues (Paunesku, Walton, Romero, Smith, Yeager, and Dweck, 2015) decided to test whether these interventions were what we call scalable. It is great to demonstrate that interventions like these are effective in a tightly controlled experiment in a small group of participants, but to what extent can we expect them to be effective if we take them for a road test in a much larger, broader sample in the messy real world?

The researchers computerized two different interventions previously demonstrated to be effective in the classroom—one inducing a growth mind-set and the other activating the purpose in learning intervention discussed earlier in this chapter. They targeted more than fifteen hundred students from thirteen different high schools. They allowed the schools to determine when and by whom the interventions would be administered, and as outcome measures they assessed end-of-term grades and successful completion of core courses. Each intervention took about forty-five minutes to complete, and involved students reading an article about the relevant intervention and then completing a writing assignment applying what they had learned to a fictional student case. A control condition involved similar reading materials and writing assignments but did not focus on mind-sets or purpose.

The results revealed that among the students most at risk of dropping out (those in the bottom third of their classes), the interventions successfully impacted their performance in core courses—their grades and their successful completion. Paunesku and colleagues raise the compelling question, "Among the 4.93 million students who constitute the lowest-performing third of high school students nationwide, could this translate into a proportional 1.18 million additional successfully completed courses?" (2015, p. 8).

It is a powerful question indeed.

PROLONGING PERSISTENCE TEACHING PRACTICE 2: REMIND YOUR STUDENTS OF THE CONTROL THEY ALREADY HAVE

Besides giving your students control over various aspects of their learning, you could also **encourage their perceived control through a brief attributional retraining or mind-set exercise**. While you likely don't have the time to create instructional videos or an extra hour in your semester to dedicate solely to a training, the sizes of the effects in the retraining studies and the sheer magnitude of the number of studies supporting the power of mind-set interventions suggest that it is worth considering how you might spend some of your class time on these efforts. For instance, before or after the first major assessment, take just ten minutes to discuss the power of attributing performance losses to poor strategizing rather than luck or teaching quality. You could ask students to complete a brief writing assignment about their emotional reactions to this first assessment and how to construct strategy-/effort-based attributions for the event.

Even less work is simply changing how you frame assessments and talk to students about what they've had success or failure with. One of the easiest and most effective ways of stimulating a growth mind-set is to **praise effort rather than ability**. Rather than telling students, "You are such a good writer!" or, "You are really skilled at completing lab reports," tell them, "You must have worked very hard on this essay!" or, "The quality of your lab report reflects how much time you must have dedicated to the effort." For other tips on activating a growth mind-set in the higher education classroom, James Lang dedicates an entire chapter of his powerful book *Small Teaching: Everyday Lessons from the Science of Learning* (2016) to a consideration of these tactics.

We can give students control, but if they don't perceive themselves as in control, that will only go so far. So remind them that they are the ones calling the shots and determining how much effort to apply to their progress in your courses.

Procrastination

All the tools mentioned so far have been great for prolonging student persistence, but even the most persistently motivated students, fully convinced of the value of your coursework and their control over their progress, are at some point going to stumble upon the roadblock of procrastination.

Imagine for a moment a world devoid of procrastination. When I do so, I am filled with a sense of unbelievable possibility:

numerous tasks are completed and skills learned, the work-day keeps to its allotted hours (because we're getting so much done!), and personal time is brought to new heights of fitness, creativity, and relaxation. While certain types of procrastination can actually be beneficial—if you're taking a short break from your work to walk the dog and then return to the work refreshed, for instance—most people report it as a net negative, bringing a decrease in productivity and an increase in negative emotions like guilt and frustration. Why, then, is procrastination so common, and so difficult to stamp out? We haven't gotten to the fifth chapter of this book without you suspecting that the answer is at least in part, of course, your emotions. Specifically, two aspects of your emotions—your natural and often reflexive impulse to down-regulate negative emotions (short-term mood repair), and the emotional and intellectual disconnect between your current and future selves.

Emotion regulation is a form of self-regulation that refers to how people manage or regulate their emotional states or the effects of these states on behavior. This sometimes effortful regulation of emotional experience is ubiquitous in daily life. Every time you successfully refrain from smirking at your child's fresh antics, run yourself a frothy bubble bath after a stressful week, or change the subject when a conversation veers into uncomfortable territory, you are regulating your emotions. We know that students frequently encounter negative emotions in the process of learning (anxiety being the most common one), so it should be no surprise that as they are tackling a difficult lab report they may take frequent breaks to turn to soothing, positive activities like texting a friend, checking in on social media, or streaming a few episodes of the latest Netflix drama.

A mysterious aspect of procrastination is that while an obvious driving contributor to it is the regulation of current negative emotions, in the long run it actually makes people feel worse—certainly by the time the task's deadline rears its ugly head, but often much sooner than that. The credits are hardly rolling on the Netflix episode by the time self-recrimination and remorse begin to wash over us. Short-term mood repair thus can't be the only contributor—unless we are really terrible regulators, which for the most part we are not. However, what we *are* terrible at is something called affective forecasting, the ability to predict how we'll feel in the future. In fact, we're generally terrible at predicting future behavior and experience in general. This is why nine out of ten of you reading this book are not saving enough for your retirement, or are telling a friend you are starting a diet and exercise program next week and actually believe that is true. Putting short-term mood repair and poor affective forecasting together, you procrastinate in the moment because it feels good, and you probably don't anticipate the strength of the negative consequences for your future self—even when your future self is mere minutes away.

Thus, the first step to combating procrastination in our students and ourselves is to understand the *why* of it, and we've tackled that pretty well—a combination of prioritization of short-term mood repair over achievement and poor affective forecasting. But what are some practical methods for helping our students to combat procrastination? Together with some collaborators, Danya Corkin, Shirley Yu, Christopher Wolters, and Margit Wiesner (2014) conducted both a literature review and a survey of 248 students (mostly freshmen) enrolled in sixteen different mathematics courses and found support for the following predictors of low levels of procrastination: (1) interest in and enjoyment of the course material; (2) teacher warmth and support, or the extent to which the teacher made students feel that he or she cared about their progress in the course; (3) high expectations for student performance and academic rigor; and (4) the extent to which the instructor provided good organization to the semester, with clear and firm deadlines. Thus, if we're serious about implementing a number of the strategies in this book, we're already at least halfway there. We spent chapter 4 considering how to maximize interest and students' sense of challenge, and chapter 3 examining how to ensure that students accurately perceive your warmth and care for their progress; in chapter 6 we'll tackle how to decrease anxiety with clear organization.

All three of these principles also fit with the idea that students procrastinate because of short-term mood repair. If our students find our classes and assignments aversive, they will need more mood repair. If we follow some of the tenets suggested by the researchers throughout this book and craft classes and assignments that are inherently interesting, challenging, and matched to our students' values, they will have less need for mood repair while working on class material. Most critically, a great deal of research suggests that procrastination increases when students perceive both the value of the material and the control they have over their work as low. If we intentionally choose learning material and activities that are interesting and valuable to our students in order to maximize attention, memory, and motivation, there should naturally be a reduction in procrastination.

Earlier in this chapter I discussed how focusing on a larger, more self-transcendent goal (e.g., running a race for charity) can yield benefits in self-control. We saw evidence for this effect in Yeager and colleagues' study on evoking self-transcendent purpose in adolescents in order to augment their persistence on boring math problems and review questions. Goal setting has been extensively studied and found to be effective for people trying to lose weight, save money, and achieve other long-term objectives. Whether goal setting might be equally effective for achieving educational goals was put to the test by Dominique Morisano, Jacob Hirsh, Jordan Peterson, Robert Pihl, and Bruce Shore (2010). This group of researchers out of McGill University recruited a sample of students who self-identified as struggling academically, and randomly assigned them to complete either a computerized set of activities focused on setting academic goals for the semester or a set focused on describing past positive experiences. This control condition (positive experiences) matched the experimental one (goal setting) on the experience of completing writing and rating tasks on a computer and on the positive tone of the exercises. Morisano and colleagues tracked all of these students over the course of the semester and found that at semester's end the goal setters had higher grade point averages, dropped fewer courses, and reported fewer negative emotions than those in the control group. Notably, when the researchers looked at the nature and quality of the goals set, the one variable that well predicted a successful semester was the number of words used in the initial free-writing exercise in which students were asked to describe their ideal semester. This suggests that the more clearly and specifically they were able to articulate their academic desires, the more effective the goal setting.[2]

Goals can improve performance by highlighting the behaviors that need to be changed and amplifying your energy to change them, but you can also give goals a giant boost with something called implementation intentions; these take the form of *if/ then* statements, and help you clearly identify the behaviors you are going to change and the contexts in which you want to change them. For instance, if you want to eat more fruits and vegetables, you might set up an implementation intention along the lines of, *If I am hungry and it is between meals,* **then** *I will choose an apple* (and then make sure you've bought some apples). Or if you want to increase your exercise you might say to yourself, **If** *it is Tuesday* *morning, **then** I will go for a run.* The more detailed and context-contingent the implementation intention, the better: ***If** it is Tuesday morning and it is pouring rain and I can't run, **then** I will go to my gym's step aerobics class instead.*

Implementation intentions may seem at face value a little cute, but they are incredibly powerful for increasing any number of goal-directed behaviors (Gollwitzer and Sheeran, 2006). They probably work via a few different mechanisms. First of all, they strengthen the link between intention and behavior by making that link explicit. Second, they identify clear, practical ways to implement the behaviors you want to change. Third, setting them requires you to examine your life and identify the various contexts and situations that prompt either the opportunity for goal-directed behavior (e.g., *Tuesday mornings are a great morning for exercise because my spouse works from home and can manage the morning shuffle with our kids*) or avenues to decrease behaviors that oppose your goal (e.g., *I snack the worst on afternoons toward the end of the week, and that's also when the fruit supply is getting low, so I'd better stop by the farm stand on my way home from work on Wednesdays*). Fourth, when you make the link between the intention and the behavior very explicit, it becomes automatic—you don't have to put a lot of effort and thinking into it, and as such it becomes a lot easier to enact. For instance, perhaps you are trying to cut down on how much alcohol you drink. Having a simple goal of drinking less is great, but having an implementation intention along the lines of ***If** I'm out to dinner and the waiter asks if I'd like another drink, **then** I'll ask for a seltzer water with lime* means that when you are in that given circumstance, the alternative response rolls off your tongue without you even needing to stop to think. Replying with your implementation intention is much easier than figuring out in the moment whether you've had "enough," what you should ask for instead, and so on.

Most of the work on implementation intentions has come out of the study of health behaviors like diet and exercise. But a few intrepid researchers have begun investigating whether they could also help students and teachers achieve their shared academic goals. For instance, Thomas Webb, Julie Christian, and Christopher Armitage (2007) examined whether setting implementation intentions would benefit class attendance. You don't need to know the research on this topic to imagine that higher class attendance predicts better grades and that struggling students are the most likely to miss class, which further hampers their performance. One of the great challenges to navigate in the transition from high school to college is the fact that as a student you are free to manage your time as you wish, and no one can make you actually attend your classes.

In Webb and colleagues' study, students from a psychology class at the University of Birmingham were randomly assigned to either set or not set implementation intentions about the *where*, *when*, and *how* of attending or not attending class (*If it is Monday morning at 9:15,* **then** *I will have a granola bar for breakfast and then walk to class*). In their analysis of the content of the implementation intentions set by students, almost half of the students used intentions that involved meeting up with friends before class. Others mentioned planned behaviors like setting an alarm or not going out the night before. Their results revealed that students who set implementation intentions attended an average of 83% of their classes, whereas students who did not set such intentions attended 69% of their classes—a difference that was statistically significant.

Implementation intentions can help with more than just attendance, however. Gabriele Oettingen and colleagues (Oettingen, Kappes, Guttenberg, and Gollwitzer, 2015; Oettingen, Pak, and Schnetter, 2001) investigated whether having students use implementation intentions in setting academic goals was more effective than control conditions in which they didn't think about their goals at all or in which they thought about their goals without setting explicit intentions. When asked to schedule their upcoming week, students who considered their ideal goal outcomes *and* set specific behavioral intentions set aside the greatest number of hours to working on goal-specific work.

PROLONGING PERSISTENCE TEACHING PRACTICE 3: EMPLOY GOAL SETTING AND DEADLINES

To decrease procrastination and help students manage their workloads, we can **use some of the tools of goal-setting science**. Following Morisano and colleagues, you could take a few minutes at the start of the semester to have students consider their academic goals for the course in a free-writing exercise.

You could also utilize implementation intentions. Based on their study, Webb and colleagues recommend **taking a few moments at the start of the semester asking students to set implementation intentions surrounding class attendance**— the *where*, *when*, and *how* of it. In addition to being a useful way for instructors to maximize student attendance in their specific courses, implementation intentions may be a useful tool in any workshops for students on academic probation or who have been identified at admission as being high-risk for low performance or dropping out.

But perhaps you already feel too crunched for class time to add non-content-related activities. If this is the case, there is another aspect of goal setting that you can implement that doesn't require class time: **frequent deadlines**. Despite Douglas Adams's humorous take on them—"I love deadlines. . . . I love the whooshing noise they make as they go by" (quoted in Wroe,

2002, p. xxiii)—deadlines are extremely effective. Most people will confess that deadlines work for them because of what happens *just before*. A few people may sit down with a calendar, break the work into even chunks, and then reliably and methodically work their way through the stack of things to be accomplished. The rest of us dash through the day-to-day minutiae of living, along the way completing the tasks with earlier deadlines until suddenly, *Oh no, **that's** due in two days*. We scramble, get down to business, and plow through the task with focus and aplomb, telling ourselves in the midst of our panic that next time we'll be one of those laudable chunk breakers instead.

That's all well and good, you might be thinking, *but we already implement deadlines; they're built right into the nature of the college classroom. Any assignment that is due has an inherent deadline—its due date.* True enough, **but I'm talking about even more frequent deadlines**. For instance, instead of distributing a handout about a large research paper due at the end of the semester and then not mentioning it again until just before you have the stack of thirty-pagers on your desk, act as the self-regulator you wish you were: make the paper topic be due in the first few weeks of class. Midway through the semester, have your students present to each other their theses and a few of their arguments or findings thus far. At around the three-quarter mark of the semester, have an informal draft due. Then have the final version due at the end of the semester. This may seem like a lot of work for you, the instructor, but if these interim assignments (such as the presentation) replace other assignments (e.g., additional papers) you may have assigned in the past, the net grading should be the same. The key is that in this framework, it is impossible for students to leave the thirty-page paper until the night before the deadline. They are forced by the very structure of the semester to spread the work out.

Chapter Summary

If you take one thing home from this chapter, it should be the importance of considering and optimizing the appraisals your students make about their assignments in your classes. To whatever extent you can, give them control of their own work, and treat them as the autonomous beings that they are. You might also take a page from attributional retraining and mind-set theory and spend some time after the first assessment reminding them that they have more control than they might think—that they can improve performance with a greater application of effort or better study strategies. Be cognizant that they are appraising, and guide them to make appraisals of the work as important to their goals, whether self-oriented, utilitarian, or self-transcendent. After all, a classroom in which students view the work as high in control and high in value is a classroom that will be filled with positive emotion and engagement, and this climate will not only enhance students' learning but make your teaching more fulfilling and enjoyable as well.

Further Reading

For a quite thorough **overview of the field of emotion regulation research**, see Gross, James J. 2013b. *Handbook of emotion regulation* (2nd ed.). New York: Guilford.

For **motivational interventions in the classroom**, see Hulleman, Chris S., and Barron, Kenn E. 2015. Motivation interventions in education: Bridging theory, research, and practice. In Lyn Corno and Eric M. Anderman (Eds.), *Handbook of educational psychology* (3rd ed., pp. 160–71). New York: Routledge.

For an overview of **the power of goal setting**, see Locke, Edwin A., and Latham, Gary P. 2002. Building a practically useful theory of goal setting and task motivation: A 35-year odyssey. *American Psychologist, 57*(9), 705–17. doi:10.1037//0003–066X.57.9.705

For more on **the power of growth mind-sets**, see Dweck, Carol S. 2006. *Mindset: The new psychology of success.* New York: Ballantine.

For specific advice on **easy ways to implement mind-set theory in your higher education classroom**, see Lang, James M. 2016. *Small teaching: Everyday lessons from the science of learning.* San Francisco: Jossey-Bass.

NOTES

1. This concept of mobilizing efforts and prolonging persistence comes from Locke and Latham's theory of goal setting (2002).

2. Or, since we can't conclude anything about causation or mechanisms based on a correlational finding, it could be that more motivated students spent more time and words on this initial visualization, and they were also the students who benefited most from goal setting, or would have had the best grades at the end of the semester regardless of goal setting.

6

BEST-LAID PLANS

When Emotions Challenge or Backfire

In the spring semester of 2015, a professor at Texas A&M University at Galveston failed his entire undergraduate management class. In his explanation for this extreme decision he stated,

> I have seen cheating, been told by students to "chill out,"
> "get out of my space," "go back and teach," refuse to leave
> the room after being told to do so following inappropriate
> conduct, called a "f****ng moron" several times by a student
> to my face. (Gumbrecht 2015)

I don't claim to know or understand what went wrong in this particular case, how a college classroom could devolve so dramatically, but I think it highlights something important that we've avoided until now. We've spent the rest of the book focused on the potential that highly charged emotions may have for student learning, but in this chapter we'll cover some of the challenges they may engender.

We've established that the classroom is a highly emotional climate, where students and teachers confront anxiety, hope, confusion, and satisfaction and where there are often high stakes. The grades students receive help determine their job prospects and which graduate or medical schools they do or do not attend. On the other hand, course evaluations by students help determine whether a junior faculty member receives tenure or whether an adjunct instructor is welcomed back to teach a sub-sequent semester. We'll begin with what is probably the best-studied emotional phenomenon in education: test anxiety. What are the contributors to anxiety in the classroom, and how can we strategize around them? We will also discuss situations in which professors and students find themselves falling into adversarial roles and how to avoid these pitfalls. Finally, we'll tackle destructive small-group dynamics and how best to assign and manage working groups in the class, and then end on a plea to practice empathy for our students, who are confronting some of the most emotional periods in their lives.

Test Anxiety

In chapter 5 we pondered how powerful manipulating appraisals of control and value can be for student motivation. But consider the setting of a job interview. Two candidates, let's call them Shona and Michael, both view the interview as high in value ("I really need this job") and high in control ("Getting this job hinges on my performance"). But they diverge in anxiety levels—Shona is quite calm, whereas Michael is fighting mounting anxiety with both physical symptoms (heart racing, palms sweating) and psychological symptoms (chronic thoughts of possible failure and its ramifications). Clearly we'd expect Shona to perform better, because anxiety has the potential to disrupt performance.

Joelle Ruthig, working with Reinhard Pekrun and others (Ruthig, Perry, Hladkyj, Hall, Pekrun, and Chipperfield, 2008), tested the possibility that negative emotions like anxiety might moderate the effects of appraisals on achievement. They followed 620 new undergraduates over the course of a year, measuring their perceived control and emotions (boredom, anxiety, and enjoyment) in the beginning of the year and their grade point average and number of credits dropped at the end of the year. The results indicated that even in the presence of a perceived high level of control, negative emotions like boredom and anxiety predicted worse performance and positive emotions like enjoyment predicted better performance. Academic emotions did not show these relationships in students with low levels of control, however, and this suggests that for those students we need to first change their sense of control and then target their emotions.

You might recall from chapter 5 that when Pekrun and colleagues studied students' emotions in the classroom, anxiety was the most frequently reported emotion, comprising up to 25% of student experiences in the classroom. Anxiety is probably so pervasive in the classroom in part because there are just so many different things to be anxious about: performance anxiety when giving group presentations, anxiety about speaking in class, anxiety about not being smart enough to master the material and, of course, anxiety about tests, quizzes, and grades.

Luckily, we know a fair bit about antecedents, causes, and how we might go about alleviating anxiety regarding tests and performance. Test anxiety appears to be made up of two, somewhat separable parts: cognition-based worry about assessment, and physiologically based emotional arousal (Bonaccio and Reeve, 2010). Most of the research on test anxiety has focused on math anxiety in particular, probably because it is quite common and because it is relatively easy to assess mathematics performance in a straightforward, objective way; it is much harder to evaluate whether students have achieved learning goals in, for instance, painting or creative writing.

In a review of the literature, Alex Moore, Amy McAuley, Gabriel Allred, and Mark Ashcraft (2014) discovered that first of all, math anxiety is a real problem: it is frequent and common, and students high in math anxiety take longer to solve problems and perform less well than students low in math anxiety. It appears to disrupt performance by hijacking part of one's working memory capacity via worrying thoughts, leaving fewer cognitive resources to direct to the problem at hand. Moore and colleagues call this an "affective drop" in performance; the non-anxious student has to juggle the task itself alongside irrelevant distractors (e.g., a phone buzzing in a pocket), but anxious students have a triple-task challenge: juggling the task, irrelevant distractors, *and* the intrusive worrying that their anxiety is producing. Research by Ian Lyons and Sian Beilock (2012) has revealed that when a subject lies in a functional magnetic resonance imaging scanner and anticipates the onset of difficult math problems, there is a relationship between levels of math anxiety and degree of brain activation in areas of the brain associated not only with the anticipation of threat but also of the actual experience of physical pain. This indicates that the highly anxious student could be in a state of not only psychological worry but also physical distress—which makes sense given that so many of the symptoms of anxiety (stomach butterflies, elevated heart rate, shivers) are physiological in nature.[1]

Consistent with this physiological arousal account, Andrew Mattarella-Micke and colleagues (Mattarella-Micke, Mateo, Kozak, Foster, and Beilock, 2011) discovered that for participants relatively high in working memory capacity, students with both low and high math anxiety exhibited greater cortisol following large math problems. It was only for the high-anxiety students that the elevated cortisol was associated with worse performance, however; in fact, for low-anxiety students, greater cortisol was associated with *better* performance. How could this be? One of the most reliable effects in the study of cognitive performance is called the Yerkes-Dodson law, named after Robert Yerkes and

John Dillingham Dodson, who originally developed the concept. It is often called the Yerkes-Dodson curve because it is literally that, a curve like a *C* lying on its open side: if you map degree of alertness/arousal/anxiety on the *x* axis and performance on the *y* axis, you'll observe that really low levels of arousal relate to low performance (because one is bored and unmotivated) and really high levels of arousal also relate to low performance (because one is an emotional wreck), but that there is a sweet spot right in the middle where one has enough arousal to be alert and engaged but also be capable of focus and concentration.

Math anxiety is particularly worrisome in our contemporary technological society because, like all forms of anxiety, it leads not only to detriments in performance but also to avoidance. Students high in math anxiety avoid mathematics courses and careers where math is involved, which could have negative effects on earning potential and mobility.

Thus, a lot is at stake. But because test-related anxiety is one of the best-studied challenges to good performance in the classroom, we also know a fair bit about how to alleviate it.

MINIMIZING AFFECTIVE CHALLENGES TEACHING PRACTICE 1: MINIMIZE TEST ANXIETY

Given how common anxiety is in higher education, and its host of negative effects on achievement and performance, strategizing it out of our classes could have a powerful effect on student learning outcomes.

First, since one of the greatest contributors to an anxiety-performance link is time pressure, doing whatever you can to **be sure students are not rushed in completing their answers** is one way to reduce test anxiety. Consider how long you think an assessment should take, and then build in some ample wiggle room. If you intend on conducting class once the assessment is finished, consider leaving a little extra time and having early finishers complete a discussion preparation worksheet so that they aren't left bored and aimless; that way, the time is still productive. It is better to have your high-anxiety students perform well on the assessment and have to play a little catch-up during discussion than have them bomb on the assessment.

Second, rather than (or in addition to) practicing mindfulness to improve your teaching presence, **think about encouraging mindfulness in your *students***. Tad Brunyé and colleagues (2013) investigated whether inducing a state of mindfulness might increase performance on a math test for participants high in math anxiety. In their research study, they asked undergraduates scoring low and high in math anxiety to complete a series of timed math tasks after engaging in focused attention on breathing, letting their minds wander, and worrying about various issues unrelated to math (e.g., cancer affecting a loved one). For the participants high in math anxiety, focused breathing was associated with higher levels of calm and better performance on the math task than were the other two conditions. While we haven't yet seen whether these effects would translate to an actual classroom scenario and to briefer interventions (the focused breathing in this study lasted fifteen minutes), leading your students in a few minutes of relaxation might have a beneficial effect on anxiety, and thus performance—even if only a minor one.

Third, you can reduce all sorts of classroom anxiety through **the practice of transparency** in your teaching methods. Anxiety arrives under conditions of uncertainty and in the perception that one might not have the skills to meet the current challenge. If our learning goals and criteria for evaluation and grading are unclear to our students, we are creating classrooms that are breeding grounds for anxiety and—even if we follow all the other advice given thus far—our students' performance will suffer.

Clear Syllabi

Thus, **aim for clarity and complete transparency in the reasoning behind your assignments, your activities, and which criteria students will be graded on**. In an essay in the *Chronicle of Higher Education*, James Lang (2015) echoes just this point after having a lengthy discussion with college tutors about information they'd like to share with professors about the problems they commonly heard from students coming in for peer tutoring. He points out that the best place to begin is with the syllabus,[2] being sure that all of this information is clearly spelled out and accessible to students from the first day of class.

An anxiety-reducing syllabus will include: (1) your learning goals for the course; (2) how specific assignments meet these learning goals; (3) a map of the lecture topics and assignment due dates; (4) a mathematical breakdown of the grading system; and (5) the correspondence between numerical grades and letter grades (this varies more than you might think). In a great example of being transparent, maximizing student autonomy, *and* reducing the number of e-mails an instructor may get in the last month of the course, teaching support coordinator Karen Huxtable-Jester shared with me a worksheet she includes in her syllabi that allows students to approximate their current grade in the course at any point in the semester. She also explained that she uses an exam analysis tool adapted from Maya Aloni of Middlesex County College in which she asks students to self-identify their stumbling blocks on the latest exam (e.g., "I didn't study the information because it wasn't in my notes," or, "This was an application problem, and it confused me") before meeting with her to discuss low exam grades (Huxtable-Jester, personal communication, November 2012). This places students in a position of control, but it also helps them reduce feelings of anxiety and helplessness after poor performance.

Clear Exams

Beyond a crystal-clear syllabus, you can most effectively reduce anxiety by targeting the heart of what makes students most anxious: testing and grading. I went to Boston University, which is a rather large institution. Because so many of my classes were giant, many of my courses had only a handful of exams carving up the semester for grade points. What this meant was that sitting down to each exam meant that I knew that a third of my final grade rode on my performance. For many students this could be truly anxiety provoking and thus disrupt performance. If you're teaching several hundred students, it may be difficult to include assignments like oral presentations or discussion leadership, but you still could **break high-stakes exams into smaller, more frequent quizzes** without increasing the net amount of grading. If you're teaching smaller courses, **explore multiple forms of grade points**. This will both reduce anxiety due to the lower stakes and also allow students with different skill sets to shine. In either format, you could also construct a course in which the **lowest exam grade is dropped**, thus taking some pressure off each exam.

Another method to reducing anxiety that works in both larger and smaller classes is to **give your students some exposure to your testing style before the day of the exam**. Quite often we instructors teach for clarity, making the concepts we're covering as digestible as possible. Students dutifully scribble down definitions and examples and then spend their study time putting these definitions and examples on flash cards, or rewriting their notes verbatim. From their perspective, they have studied like mad for

our exams. Yet we don't care that they know word-for-word definitions or the specific examples we used while lecturing. We
construct our exams for application, to test that students understand the underlying theories or processes that we have labored
hard to teach them. We see this as good teaching and good testing, but students see this as a nasty trick we've played on them.
Of course, we don't want to stop testing for understanding and
creative application of knowledge, but what we can do is make
sure that students see examples of how they'll be evaluated
before they study, so that they know *how* to study.

I recently employed this tactic in my Introduction to Psychology course. I had previously had five exams spread throughout the semester, but that was honestly a lot of class time used
up, and a lot of grading, and I was hearing from students on
course evaluations that they also felt it was too much. I decided
to test out a three-exam semester (and yes, I do have other
assignments besides exams, so each exam doesn't carry terribly
high stakes). I worried, however, that the reduced frequency of
exams would hurt student grades. In my past experience a subset
of students do terribly on the first exam, come to see me in office
hours to discuss study strategies, and subsequently improve.
With fewer exams worth more points, I worried that waiting so
long until the first exam could negatively impact their performance. For this reason, I have since implemented something I
call "group quizzes." I administer two group quizzes between
exams. Each quiz consists of three multiple-choice questions that
students answer together in small groups during the first ten
minutes of class. I implement these quizzes primarily so that students will know what my multiple-choice questions look like well
before exams and thus reduce anxiety by increasing clarity, but
they also achieve several other learning goals. First, they identify
for the students the material I find most important for each
subsection of the course. Second, they prompt students to begin

talking with each other. Perhaps it was a coincidence, but the first semester I implemented group quizzes, I noticed a much higher degree of student interaction and enthusiastic discussions across a number of activities. Third, they served as an excellent small-scale review that helped students to grapple with the material we had learned in the previous class or two.

Clear Written and Oral Assignments

Of course, not all courses use exams, and most courses don't only use exams. How can we grade papers, presentations, and other more subjective assignments while keeping in mind clarity and a reduction in anxiety? I would argue that grading for clarity is even more important for these types of assignments, as the "shrouded-in-mystery" effect is even more salient. On exams, students can see that there is one correct answer that they didn't circle or write down on the free response. But for students writing a paper or giving an oral presentation, the difference between an A and a B, or a B and a C, is relatively obscure. Thus, try to be as transparent as possible about what you expect—again, *before* the assignment is due. Use grading rubrics that break down for students exactly where they are earning and losing points (consider including both discrepancy feedback and progress feedback, as discussed in chapter 4). **Consider distributing your grading rubric before the first assignment is due.** If for any reason this makes you uncomfortable, at least hand out a list of criteria on which your students will be graded.

A great transparency practice suggested by James Lang in his book *On Course: A Week-by-Week Guide to Your First Semester of College Teaching* (2010) is to **share examples of what an A assignment would look like for any grade point you're assigning.** Are you asking students to write a research paper? Give them a mock one that would receive high marks. Are you asking them to give a five-minute presentation? Demonstrate a few examples that incorporate all the criteria on your grading rubric.

All of these are techniques that should reduce student anxiety and thus allow your other efforts to increase students' perceived control and value to effectively improve not just motivation but also performance.

Justice, Injustice, and the Struggle for Power

In the context of higher education, instructors are making frequent bids for student time and attention, and this restricts students' freedom. The introduction of large assignments or upcoming deadlines restricts how students will spend their leisure time. Instructors are also setting rules and regulations for classroom behavior and devising course assignments and grading rubrics that will help determine student progress in their current degree program, as well as their future prospects for employment or graduate study. Thus, the higher education classroom is rife with potential power struggles that may engender negative emotions. Indeed, one of the most common elicitors of negative emotions in students arises when they perceive an unjust infraction against their freedom, and the emotions they experience can be rather intense. Students who are asked how they feel in response to perceptions of classroom injustice report feeling angry, pained, frustrated, powerless, stressed, violated, cheated, disgusted, and embarrassed (Chory, Horan, Carton, and Houser, 2014). Researchers call responses of this type "psychological reactance," defined by Qin Zhang and David Sapp as "the psychological, emotional, or motivational state aroused when a perceived behavioral freedom is threatened, reduced, or eliminated" (2013, p. 1).

Psychological reactance in the classroom is a troublesome phenomenon, because it can result in students attempting to regain their threatened freedom and autonomy by rebelling. They may flout your requests, refuse to participate in class discussions, engage in academic dishonesty, or actively or passively demonstrate disrespect. Reactance can be particularly problematic if students begin to share their disgruntlement with each other and encourage each other to greater heights of rebellion. These group effects can be even stronger in classes where the students share relationships outside the classroom, as when students participate in learning communities, as is often the case in first-year programs. This effect has been called "hyperbonding" (Watts, 2013). In these instances, the processes of group dynamics can result in the students sharing a cohort and a group identity separate from that of the instructor, which limits the instructor's ability to influence the students during the very first days of class.

The instructor's power in the classroom stems from several sources: (1) coercive/reward power, meting out punishments and granting rewards; (2) legitimate power, as the classroom is set up with the expectation that the instructor holds the power; (3) expert power, yielded when the students perceive the instructor as holding expertise they do not currently have; and (4) referent power, practiced only when the students like and respect the instructor. Julie Watts (2013) has reviewed decades of literature on types of enacted power in the higher education classroom and which types are associated with good outcomes. She claims that the best outcomes are associated with uses of power in which the instructor de-emphasizes coercive or legitimate power and maximizes reward, expert, and referent power. The research she reviews supports the idea that behaviors like developing rapport, making eye contact, expressing respect for students, and caring about their learning outcomes are all associated with good classroom outcomes. We'll revisit these and some other tips on reducing reactance later in this chapter.

These struggles of power and potential reactance can arise in any classroom, regardless of the subject matter or the personal characteristics of the instructor standing at the head of the class. But, of course, classrooms are also microcosms of their larger societies, and thus are sadly not at all exempt from the dynamics of implicit bias, prejudice, and privilege that are threaded throughout experience. The ongoing tug of war for power and control between students and instructor is going to vary with the age, gender, ethnicity, and sexual orientation of the instructor.

For instance, let's consider the specific case of teaching as a faculty member of color. In an analysis of interviews with black and white professors teaching in a large, predominantly white university, Roxanna Harlow (2003) found that 76% of black professors reported that their students questioned their qualifications, competency, and credibility, whereas only 7% of white professors reported the same, despite the groups being matched on status and discipline. The black professors also frequently discussed ways that they consciously managed students' perceptions of their credibility, such as presenting themselves in an authoritative manner or starting class with one's credentials, and that they felt a strong pressure to make no mistakes in order to avoid confirming stereotypes about their race or raising questions in students' minds about whether they were "an affirmative action hire." In stark contrast, white professors (especially white male professors) were so assured of student perceptions of their competence and credibility that they often discussed ways of being self-deprecating to increase student comfort.

In a startling anecdote, one black female professor offered that a white male student didn't believe something she was teaching. Rather than asking her to elaborate or support her argument, after class he sought out a white male colleague of hers to confirm the information, and then returned to inform her that, as it turned out, she was right after all. These challenges to authority can take an even uglier turn than the condescension and disrespect illustrated in this anecdote. Chavella Pittman (2010) qualitatively analyzed interviews performed with seventeen women faculty members of color and found that they frequently reported experiencing hostile challenges to their authority—nearly unilaterally at the hands of white male students. Disturbingly, many of the faculty reported feeling intimidated by the implicit or explicit aggressiveness that sometimes accompanied these challenges.

While a consideration of how not only race but also age, gender, ethnicity, sexual orientation, and class might influence perceptions of credibility and authority, openness to instruction, reactance, hostility, bias in course evaluations and so on is beyond the scope of this book, Kim Case's *Deconstructing Privilege: Teaching and Learning as Allies in the Classroom* (2013) and Kerry Ann Rockquemore and Tracey Laszloffy's *The Black Academic's Guide to Winning Tenure—Without Losing Your Soul* give a deeper consideration of some of these topics. Other than dismantling the structural disparities in our society and the hidden (and not-so-hidden) assumptions about competence saturating our media and public discourse, this is not a problem with an easy answer.

The best solution is probably some help from our friends in administration. Writing in the NEA Higher Education Journal, Frank Tuitt and colleagues recommend that

> the academy identify new models for creating institutional change; pay attention to the climate and conditions under which faculty of color teach; and signal to faculty of color that PWIs [predominantly white institutions] are invested

in their growth, development, and success by doing everything possible to ensure that support and resources are
available. Then and only then will teaching while Black and
Brown cease to feel like teaching in the line of fire. (Tuitt,
Hanna, Martinez, Salazar, and Griffin, 2009, p. 73)

MINIMIZING AFFECTIVE CHALLENGES TEACHING PRACTICE 2: AVOID REACTANCE AND HYPERBONDING

Psychological reactance, hyperbonding, and classroom incivilities arise in part because of inherent imbalances of power in the
classroom. But we can't escape the fact that the very nature of
this relationship is one where the instructor holds power over
the students—in terms of structuring the class activities, assigning tasks and deadlines, and managing the overall flow of the
course.

So how can we reduce reactance?

Some of the advice Zhang and Sapp (2013) share from two
research studies and a review of the literature includes **using
language that is low in threat or demands, expressing empathy
and interpersonal similarity, and employing those immediacy cues** that also contribute to a perception of optimism. They
demonstrate that reactance is less likely in circumstances in
which the teacher is perceived as polite and credible, when the
requests are perceived as legitimate (e.g., making sense in terms
of the course goals), and when students feel they have a close
relationship with the instructor.

It is fascinating to note that in Zhang and Sapp's research,
the effect of these variables on student resistance was not a direct
one—the variables affected resistance by way of reactance.
Stated in simpler terms, politeness and credibility predicted that
the students would experience fewer negative emotions and

perceptions of threats to their freedom, which then predicted a lower degree of plans to enact resistance. It was the emotions that mattered. As Zhang and Sapp note,

> An impolite and/or illegitimate request by a less credible teacher in a distant teacher/student relationship is more likely to incur reactance and negative attitudes, which in turn triggers more resistance, than a polite and/or legitimate request by a credible teacher in a close teacher/student relationship. (2013, p. 18)

These findings echo Watts's (2013) review of hyperbonding in student groups: **practicing immediacy, transparency, and engagement** in your classes is your best strategy for avoiding the formation of destructive group dynamics. Watts emphasizes that it is easier to prevent hyperbonding than to dismantle it once it has developed; thus, paying attention to the power dynamics of the classroom and developing relationships with your students through prosocial mechanisms of power and influence pays off the most when you do so during the first days of class. She claims that the best outcomes are associated with uses of power in which the instructor de-emphasizes coercive or legitimate power and maximizes reward, expertise, and referent power. **Recall that the classroom is a microcosm of life, and that as much as you should care about the work of the class, you also need to attend to its social dynamics (Howard, 2015).**

Watts also notes that on occasions where hyperbonding has already occurred—perhaps some of your students share a dormitory with each other, or have previously had classes together—your repertoire of power strategies is limited, because these students may have developed relationships (bonding) that result in them being less open to your attempts to develop relationships with them (bridging). While these ideas have not yet been empirically tested, she suggests that in cases where hyperbonding has already occurred, it may be advantageous to **acknowledge and strategize around the fact that the students have already built a cohort and know each other better than they know you.** She suggests such activities as having students create and circulate learning portfolios of past work so that the instructor can quickly get to know them both individually and collectively. She also proposes that in cases of learning communities such as shared dorms, the administration may want to assign advocates who will serve as an intermediary between the student group and their instructors. Echoing many other discussions in the present volume, Watts also encourages transparency and good teaching practices, such as immediacy and the development of relationships. On the transparency side, she suggests building into the course some opportunities for both the students and the instructor to reflect and direct student learning in groups—to make explicit the role of the group dynamics in the course.

Thus, paying attention to the quality of your relationship with your students, taking the time to explain the legitimacy of your assignments and how they relate to course goals, and employing some good old-fashioned politeness can go a long way in managing how students perceive your requests of them.

Social Loafing in Small-Group Activities

For most of this book, we've been treating students as individuals who are working in isolation. This is the case much of the time: they take assessments primarily on their own, and very often perform much of their work on their own. But instructors also frequently break classes into small groups to have students complete discussions, work together on a short activity during class hours, or put together a presentation that is later performed in front of the entire class. Therefore, we would be remiss to ignore the impact of group dynamics on emotions and motivations in the classroom.

The motivation behind small-group collaboration seems to be an assumption that assigning students to work together results in heightened enjoyment, motivation, and/or learning. It also is one of the few things that we do routinely in higher education that seems immediately translatable to a work environment—few and far between are the jobs our students will go on to get that won't require working cooperatively with others to accomplish tasks or solve problems. Yet anyone who has ever worked in a small group knows that it is rare that the entire group works seamlessly together, sharing the effort equally. As one viral tweet put it, "When I die, I want my group project members to lower me into my grave . . . so that they can let me down one more time."

Consulting social psychology reveals potential support for either of these possibilities—group projects could enhance or disrupt motivation. On the positive side, as we considered in chapter 3, the need to feel related or socially embedded in a shared human enterprise is a fundamental motivational drive, so group assignments should be more enjoyable and motivating than individual assignments. These positive emotions should correspondingly enhance attention and memory and result in better learning. On the other hand, a rich literature supports the idea that when people are placed in groups, social loafing and division of responsibility often occurs. These social processes likely result in undue burden on the group members who are conscientious, allowing other group members to float without doing work. So which is it? Does group work increase or decrease motivation?

Kosha Bramesfeld and Karen Gasper (2010) examined the interactions of mood and group efforts on performance in university students. Their expectations were that working collectively and current mood state may independently and interactively contribute to higher or lower distraction, loafing, and/or engagement. They manipulated college student participants to either be in a happy or sad mood using film clips, then told them to read a murder mystery and answer a number of questions regarding character guilt and how they came to these decisions. Participants were further told that they would eventually be coming to a final decision either individually or with a group (though no one actually ever worked together). Their results indicated that when people anticipated making a decision on their own, those who were feeling sad performed better and worked more analytically—which is something that replicates past research. As it turns out, happy people aren't great decision makers—they tend to rely on glossy overviews and rules of thumb. Yet these results didn't hold for those who anticipated working in a group. When people anticipated making a collective decision, it was those in happy moods who became more engaged—applying greater effort and experiencing, in association, a better performance.

Moreover, in their review of the previous literature, Bramesfeld and Grasper found that the factors that predict social loafing include circumstances with simple tasks, masked contributions (that is, the grader cannot discern individual contributions to the group effort), and those in which group members share the belief that there is not a "correct" answer. If students perceive that you are asking them to labor for the sake of laboring (to undertake "busy work"), they will be most likely to loaf.

Reading this over, you may be thinking what I am thinking—that yet again, it is all about appraisals. Avoiding social loafing in your group assignments means managing how your students appraise or interpret their own contributions to the project as well as the inherent challenge level and value of the assignment.

But group work often falls short of expectations not just because of the social loafers or so-called free riders but also because some students fail to contribute because they are struggling with the material and don't understand *how* to contribute. These students may also worry that if they take ownership of part of the project, they will complete their portion poorly or incorrectly; they may thus assume it is better to loaf than to make active errors and harm the group's grade. Sadly, but perhaps not surprisingly, case studies illustrate that fellow students lack the skills to differentiate between free riders and struggling group members and thus tend to penalize both with such behaviors as assigning them parts of the project that are most onerous and that often don't fit their skill sets (e.g., put the shy student in charge of contacting outside sources; Freeman and Greenacre, 2011).

It seems that having students work in groups has several pitfalls (loafing, penalizing struggling students, etc.), but thankfully there are strategies around these pitfalls that we'll review next. Because as we've seen earlier in this section, as well as throughout this book, tapping into social motivations can be quite powerful—as can mixing up your daily class routines to minimize boredom.

MINIMIZING AFFECTIVE CHALLENGES TEACHING PRACTICE 3: CIRCUMVENT SOCIAL LOAFING

One of the best ways to minimize social loafing and thus optimize small-group effectiveness is to enhance appraisals of control, value, and challenge for all of your students. Thus, employing all of the strategies we've reviewed thus far when designing group work as well as individual work is the first best step to effective group work. Simply sticking students in groups does not automatically make for a valuable, active learning assignment. To maximize student appraisals of value, **be sure that your motivation for assigning the work is clear**. Which learning goals is the group work fulfilling? Since group work is by definition social, and there will be a certain level of performance anxiety introduced, **be sure that the correct answer or appropriate performance is transparent to the students** and they know what good work looks like. Work that is graded or otherwise evaluated will enhance students' sense that the work is valuable and will contribute to their progress in the course.

Given the possible vicious cycle of struggling students being penalized with destructive actions like leaving them off group e-mails and assigning them overly onerous tasks (Freeman and Greenacre, 2011), it is important to **counsel the students about the best process through which to delegate tasks** as well as the importance of matching tasks to a person's skill set. Any guidance you can offer in terms of best practices to your students will be helpful.

Give your students the tools to monitor their own progress and correct for problems. Approaches to this vary, but can include **daily diaries of progress or weekly progress e-mails to the instructor**. These tools can not only raise awareness within the group of adaptive and maladaptive dynamics but can also be an early warning system for you, the instructor. Wherever possible, you want to give the groups autonomy, but there may be cases where you need to intervene with some advice or course correction. **If you do need to intervene, research suggests that the best interventions** (1) target the student(s) with destructive behavior, (2) phrase the intervention as focused on the problem behavior (every parent knows this trick: "You aren't bad, you just made some bad choices"), and (3) focus on the benefits to the group as a whole so as to motivate prosocial behavior (Freeman and Greenacre, 2011). The student might not care about his or her personal grade, but feeling responsible for the group members' grades might be motivating.

Donald Bacon, Kim Stewart, and William Silver (1999) assessed management students' self-reports of the characteristics of their best and worst group assignment experiences and distilled them into a **series of recommendations for assigning group work successfully**. These included: (1) providing clear descriptions of the group work and assignment expectations (detailed, in writing, and with a grading sheet wherever possible); (2) maximizing team longevity (longer-working teams result in better experiences); (3) whenever possible, allowing for self-selected groups, or at least polling students as to perceived skills and preferred team members before engaging in group selection; and (4) not using end-of-term peer assessments. Notably, Bacon and colleagues found that these end-of-term peer assessments were associated with poorer group dynamics. They speculate that knowing that the feedback is coming allows students to neglect addressing problematic dynamics during the process, feeling that they'll have their chance to "burn" the loafing student at the end of term. The authors instead encourage repeated, segmented feedback or doing away with peer evaluation all together.

Emotional Soup

Inevitably, my most successful teaching week of the spring semester co-occurs with Valentine's Day. This has nothing to do with the dreary New England weather offering few alternatives vying for my students' attention or the cognitive benefits of their heightened chocolate consumption. Rather, it has to do with the fact that we talk about romantic love in most of my psychology courses, and in my experience there are few other topics that arrest the attention of college students to the same degree. In my Motivation and Emotion course, I lead with a story about an argument I once had with one of my closest friends and collaborators.

Essentially, we had a pressing deadline for a conference that was happening in a few scant weeks in Berlin, and no time in which to do the work. I had just begun a tenure-track position and thus was teaching four new courses while setting up a research laboratory for the first time, all with only part-time child care for my toddler. My collaborator was a graduate student newly in the thrall of first love.

One crisp fall day I traveled to my friend's lab. We had a single hour to meet and figure out how to get everything done under the deadline. However, he had been separated from his new beloved for a good part of the morning and wanted to use the first fifteen minutes of our precious hour to go visit her in her laboratory upstairs. We fought about this, and I won: he stayed put. But for the duration of our meeting he was distracted, tense, and outright jittery, acting for all the world like a coffee addict needing his fix. I eventually threw up my hands and decided the work would get done another day.

I tell this story in my Motivation and Emotion class because it illustrates several important characteristics not just of romantic love but of emotion in general. I tell this story here for a very different reason. We have spent most of this book focused on how as educators we can utilize the power of emotion to motivate our students and help them learn better, longer, and more deeply. Yet, like many powerful tools, emotions can be double-edged; they can actually disrupt learning. One way in which this can happen, and which my friend in love experienced, is through the competing emotional landscape that is the life of students outside the classroom. If emotions related to a simple classroom activity can transform education to the extent that students' overall grade point averages at the end of the semester are affected, then just imagine what an effect losing a parent, or being isolated from one's social group, or falling in love could have. Emotions related to such powerful life outcomes can dominate a student's focus completely.

Just how emotional are the lives of our students? A substantial body of work now supports the idea that older people (you, reading this book, and others, even later in life) are generally much happier and more content than much younger people (the students we teach). Why is this? There are multiple possible reasons, but the theory gaining the most support has to do with the fact that as mortality looms, people prioritize their happiness more than when they are young, when their lives seem to spread out into the distance ahead (Carstensen, 1992). As an older adult, you are likely to cull down your social network to focus on your deepest connections; you might stop trying to adhere to the latest fashions and trends and instead follow your heart; you might spend more time doing the things that reward you. In contrast, younger people prioritize new experiences, new adventures, and the building of social relationships for the future—whether or not those relationships are deeply close. They are also exquisitely aware of how their behavior, dress, and activities are either in or out of tune with current societal trends. It isn't hard to see how the former priorities might yield more contentment and positive emotions than the latter ones.

This is called the socioemotional selectivity theory, pioneered by Laura Carstensen, and it is a dominant theory of age differences in emotion. Quite apart from older people prioritiz-ing things that make them happy, another major difference between youth and older age is the uncertainty that youth brings. College-age students are still trying to determine what they find rewarding, and what a deep connection means to them. As a college student, you most often don't know what your career will be, where you'll live, what kind of income bracket you'll be in, whether you'll marry or have children; that open road spread-ing out before you can be exciting, but it can also be pretty damned intimidating. Moreover, we know from other research that uncertainty is linked with negative emotions. Indeed, anxi-ety is an affective experience that is almost entirely defined by uncertainty, and anxiety disorders are the most commonly diag-nosed form of mental duress in our country.

Moreover, substantial data suggest that novel experiences are more emotional: the first time someone breaks your heart; the first time someone you trust rejects you in front of others; or the first time you pour your very best into a body of work and your mentor finds it lacking. Our students are in one of the most highly uncertain times in their lives, filled with novel expe-riences that they haven't yet developed the tools to manage and thrown into a new environment with entirely new people and new systems they don't yet understand. Moreover, they are also in a time of life in which they are beginning and ending roman-tic liaisons with greater frequency than at any other time of life.

Our students, in essence, are simmering in a giant vat of emotional soup, and it is a soup that most of us teaching them, advising them, and policing their performance and behavior can barely recall.

MINIMIZING AFFECTIVE CHALLENGES TEACHING
PRACTICE 4: BE EMPATHETIC

In terms of trying to combat the numerous and often over-whelming emotional priorities our students experience, I'm afraid there is not much I can suggest in the way of actions to take; our students are in this soup for better or for worse, and the only way through it is through it. But I do think it is important for us, as educators, to appreciate the dizzying emotional complexity and competing priorities of our students' lives—both in tempering our expectations for how arresting our classroom demonstrations might be and in deciding how forgiving to be of lapses in motivation or performance. There are going to be days that no matter how much singing and dancing we do, they'll be wrapped up in their own internal universes. And while we always want to encourage responsibility and accountability, **generating a little empathy** for the usually excellent student asking for an extension on a paper because of a (seemingly trivial, in your mind) fight with a roommate may go an extra mile in supporting his or her educational progress. Or as digital teacher and pedagogue Sean Michael Morris reflects on his blog after an inspiring pedagogical institute he attended:

> Love in pedagogical work is an orientation. It's a commit-ment to the personhood of learners, to their intersectionality, to their deep emotional backgrounds, to the authenticity of their lives. It is a decision to commit first to the community of learners and second to the material we've come to teach. When we speak about love in pedagogical work, we suspend our habitual talk about assessment, content, educational technology, plagiarism, compliance. We do not need to eliminate that talk, but when we return to it after orienting ourselves to a pedagogy of care, it is no longer

habitual talk—it is considered discussion, that often includes the learner. Love gives rise to the critical in this way, for it demands the decay of unconsidered habit. (2016)

It is also a good idea to **be knowledgeable about our institutions' offerings in terms of providing emotional support** to the student body. Know where the counseling office is, and how to get in touch with it. Many schools also have committees dedicated to being on the watch for student welfare issues that may arise; be sure to know how to get in touch with these folks as well. If you have students who are exhibiting signs of emotional struggle, utilize these resources. Students will have the best emotional experience in your classroom if they're experiencing emotional stability outside it.

Chapter Summary

This has not been an exhaustive list of the emotional pitfalls that can arise in the classroom, but hopefully you now have a series of strategies in place to avoid some of the most common problems. Recall that your students' understanding of the material and experiences in the classroom are at a much different level of reality than your own. In grading, be as clear as you can about your expectations, your criteria, and how students' actual work will be translated into a resulting number or letter grade. Assign group work as thoughtfully as you do individual work, and hold students individually accountable for their contributions to the group.

Finally, doing what you can to utilize some of the positive effects of emotion in the classroom, as discussed in chapters 3–5, will avoid many of the other potential problems that can crop up.

Maximizing optimism will minimize frustration and despair; maximizing interest will minimize boredom; maximizing appraisals of control and value will minimize lack of motivation and anxiety.

As they say, the best defense is a good offense.

Further Reading

For a thorough **review of the applied study of social mechanics in the classroom**, see Cozolino, Louis. 2013. *The social neuroscience of education: Optimizing attachment and learning in the classroom*. New York: Norton.

For a **quite thorough review of decades of research on test anxiety**, see Moore, Alex M., McAuley, Amy J., Allred, Gabriel A., and Ashcraft, Mark H. 2014. Mathematics anxiety, working memory, and mathematical performance: The triple-task effect and the affective drop in performance. In Steve Chinn (Ed.), *The Routledge international handbook of dyscalculia and mathematical learning difficulties* (pp. 326–36). Abingdon, England: Routledge.

For more on the **changes in emotion over the lifespan**, see Urry, Heather L., and Gross, James J. 2010. Emotion regulation in older age. *Current Directions in Psychological Science, 19*(6), 352–57. http://doi.org/10.1177/0963721410388395

NOTES

1. Here we need to be careful not to commit the neuroscience sin of "reverse inference"; just because these areas are activated in anticipation of math doesn't directly mean that the participants are experiencing physical pain. Brain areas involved in one experience tend to be involved in many other experiences, and we can't conclude

anything about the lived experiences of the participants without asking them or using other, converging methodologies.

2. Of course, the easiest joke to make among academics is to poke fun at students' seeming inability to read the syllabi; clear syllabi will only go so far. Or, as the humorous Twitter account Shit Academics Say puts it, "There are no stupid questions. On an unrelated topic, the course syllabus is still available online, by email, and in hard copy."

CONCLUSION

In the introduction to this book I related a story about my favorite teacher. Now I'd like you to call to mind your favorite *fictional* teacher—someone from a novel or film.

Take a moment—I'll wait.

I'm guessing that, among a scattering of Albus Dumbledores and Jenny Calendars, quite a number of you nominated John Keating from the film *Dead Poets Society*—a charismatic, energetic English instructor brought to vibrant life by a young Robin Williams. Keating exemplifies many of the characteristics and techniques we've been discussing throughout this book. He is active and enthusiastic. He shouts and quotes Walt Whitman, and demands that his students stand on their desks while reciting poetry. He frequently employs humor. He is optimistic and supportive, and profoundly cares about his students' progress and well-being. ("Make your lives extraordinary!" he shouts). He employs unconventional, role-playing techniques to harness his students' attention, direct it to the material at hand, and make it their own.

In addition, he also profoundly understands that to make his material interesting and important to these young men who are distracted by their own concerns he needs to manipulate their appraisals of value and control. He manipulates control by encouraging them to develop their own methods of critiquing poetry (indeed, having them rip out the part of their textbook that suggests a restrictive, formulaic approach) and by encouraging them to form their own poetry society, where they meet in a cave to read and write poems.

In addition to the automatic value added by control, Keating also brings a transcendent purpose to the material:

> We don't read and write poetry because it's cute. We read and write poetry because we are members of the human race. And the human race is filled with passion. And medicine, law, business, engineering, these are noble pursuits and necessary to sustain life. But poetry, beauty, romance, love, these are what we stay alive for.

While the film is fictional, its portrayal of an inspirational teacher shares many commonalities with *other* inspirational teachers from books and films, some of whom are fictionalized portrayals of real-life people, such as Edward James Olmos's character in *Stand and Deliver.* And like any good fiction, it resonates with us because it echoes our own lived experiences: the teachers who truly teach us, move us, and change us are those who convey what Melanie Keller and colleagues call a "contagious fire" (Keller, Goetz, Becker, Morger, and Hensley, 2014, p. 29). In this book I have made the argument that we can employ techniques suggested by the behavioral and neuroscientific study of emotion and motivation to light such a fire.

We have reviewed quite a number of studies and examined quite a lot of advice. My hope is that this book will serve as a resource you can return to when you encounter a particular emotional challenge in the classroom. Are you teaching an introductory mathematics course to students who haven't met the admissions benchmark for math proficiency, and thus you are peering over the lectern at a group of grumpy, reluctant learners? Turn to chapter 4 for some ideas on how to trigger interest and engagement. Does your Introduction to Western Civilization class seem to be populated with students who are interested in the material but have trouble following through? Review some of the prolonging persistence advice in chapter 5. Do you sense that your organic chemistry students seem to be banding together against you as a perceived enemy? Flip to chapter 6 and some of the advice there on how to avoid or dismantle destructive power dynamics in the classroom.

Perhaps you are engaged by the book's central thesis, not facing a particular problem, and want to kick-start your new semester. If this is the case, it might be helpful to distill some of the advice herein down to some core ideas or central themes that cross several areas of pedagogical research.

Without further ado:

Choosing activities, readings, and assignments that are interesting, self-relevant, emotionally evocative, and/or deeply relevant to the future careers of students may be the most powerful organizing principle you have as a teacher. I came to the writing of this book as an affective scientist deeply interested and versed in that literature. I felt that the primary work of writing this book would be the review of basic affective science and making the case that these principles should hold relevance for the classroom. While we need quite a bit of additional research, I was nonetheless delighted to find in the education literature a wealth of data already suggesting the many ways in which emotions impact learning. Combined with the basic science, such literature supports the case that if you want to capture the attention, harness the working memory, bolster the long-term retention, and enhance the motivation of your students, considering the emotional impact of various aspects of your course design is one of the best approaches you can take. This is what we might expect from the basic science of how our nervous systems have evolved, but such science has also been handsomely demonstrated in actual classrooms, where activities that consider emotions yield better performance than activities that do not, and where students experiencing high levels of activating positive emotions and low levels of negative deactivating ones outperform those students with the reverse set of experiences.

Practicing full transparency will yield benefits in motivation, heighten student perception of your supportiveness and honesty, decrease student anxiety, and alleviate psychological reactance. A recurring theme I observed across multiple bodies of research was the idea that being as transparent as you can be is associated with a host of important pedagogical outcomes. By *transparent*, I mean discussing with your students, and writing out in the syllabus and other handouts (1) your goals for the course, (2) what they can hope to learn, (3) how each of your assignments and assessments meets these learning goals, (4) your expectations for good performance on assessments, and (5) how they will be graded. Discuss these aspects of the course early and often. Practicing transparency will increase students' perceptions of the value of the activities and assignments and thereby increase motivation, decrease ambiguity (and thus anxiety), and alleviate any power struggles that may arise.

Teaching is a performance profession, so hone your performance: transmit confidence, curiosity, optimism, and immediacy in your verbal and nonverbal performance. "Teaching is a performance profession" is a quote from Doug Lemov, whose work we visited in chapter 4. Lemov was teaching in the Boston public school system and having difficulty maintaining the interest and attention of his students. As someone with an MBA and a generally analytic mind, he decided to try to codify the attributes of good teachers. To do so, he began to catalog those schools that were achieving the best academic records despite working with students from impoverished (and thus challenged) backgrounds. He visited these schools and videotaped the teachers with the best records, then analyzed the videotapes for common practices and attributes. He published these results in the book *Teach Like a Champion 2.0* (2015). Even though many of the practices he suggests are targeted at elementary and secondary school teachers rather than those of us in higher education, the book is nonetheless a fascinating read, and full of great ideas for managing classroom life moment by moment. His close study of the most effective teachers involves many of the kinds of behaviors we discussed in chapter 3 and supports his thesis that teaching is a performance profession.

In higher education there is sometimes resistance to this idea that teaching should have anything to do with performance. Some people hold the view that if you are a learned scholar in a field, that should be enough to make you a good teacher. But as an instructor you are an expert in front of a passive audience of students, tasked with holding their attention and presenting them with a variety of visual and auditory stimuli that you hope will move them. Like it or not, you are a performer. Paying attention to practices like how much eye contact you are making, to what degree you are mixing up your vocal tone or using gestures, and how much enthusiasm and positivity you are portraying with your word choice and energy level will all go quite a long way. One of my professor friends once confessed, "Sometimes it seems to me that all that matters is how much they like you. If they like you, they'll work hard and forgive you anything. If they don't like you, you can't do anything right." This was a confession, said in a hushed voice, because we shouldn't care about how much our students like us—we are authority figures, experts, not elementary school classmates. We shouldn't care, that is, unless how much they like us determines how much attention they'll pay, how much effort they'll expend in the class, and how open they will be to our instruction. Because if how much they like us determines how much they learn, likability suddenly seems a lot more important.

Writer, mythologist, and influential thinker Joseph Campbell reportedly once said, "The job of an educator is to teach students to see the vitality in themselves." I would humbly add that we also need to teach students to see the vitality in what we're teaching them. As it turns out, we have already evolved complex and powerful systems for detecting and prioritizing that which is vital. They are the emotions, and they deserve to be at the top of your pedagogical tool kit.

REFERENCES

Admiraal, Wilfried, Huizenga, Jantina, Akkerman, Sanne, and ten Dam, Geert. 2011. The concept of flow in collaborative game-based learning. *Computers in Human Behavior, 27*(3), 1185–94. doi:10.1016/j.chb.2010.12.013

Ambady, Nalini, and Rosenthal, Robert. 1993. Half a minute: Predicting teacher evaluations from thin slices of nonverbal behavior and physical attractiveness. *Journal of Personality and Social Psychology, 64*(3), 431–41.

Bacon, Donald R., Stewart, Kim A., and Silver, William S. 1999. Lessons from the best and worst student team experiences: How a teacher can make the difference. *Journal of Management Education, 23*(5), 467–88. doi:10.1177/105256299902300503

Bain, Ken. 2011. *What the best college teachers do.* Cambridge, MA: Harvard University Press.

Banas, John A., Dunbar, Norah, Rodriguez, Dariela, and Liu, Shr-Jie. 2011. A review of humor in educational settings: Four decades of research. *Communication Education, 60*(1), 115–44. doi:10.1080/0363 4523.2010.496867

Barrett, Lisa Feldman, with Barrett, Daniel J. 2015, July 5. Brain scientist: How Pixar's "Inside Out" gets one thing deeply wrong. *WBUR's Common Health.* Retrieved from http://commonhealth .wbur.org/2015/07/brain-scientist-how-pixars-inside-out-gets-one -thing-deeply-wrong

Bechara, Antoine, Damasio, Hanna, and Damasio, Antonio R. 2000. Emotion, decision making and the orbitofrontal cortex. *Cerebral Cortex, 10*(3), 295–307.

Becker, Eva Susann, Goetz, Thomas, Morger, Vinzenz, and Ranellucci, John. 2014. The importance of teachers' emotions and instructional behavior for their students' emotions: An experience-sampling analysis. *Teaching and Teacher Education, 43*, 15–26. doi:10.1016/j.tate.2014.05.002

Beckes, Lane, Coan, James A., and Hasselmo, Karen. 2013. Familiarity promotes the blurring of self and other in the neural representation of threat. *Social Cognitive and Affective Neuroscience, 8*(6): 670–77. doi: 10.1093/scan/nss046

Berk, Ronald A. 2014. "Last professor standing!": PowerPoint enables all faculty to use humor in teaching. Retrieved from http://www.ronberk.com/articles/2014_HumorFinal.pdf

Blackwell, Lisa Sorich. (n.d.). Create a growth mindset culture and increase student achievement. Retrieved from http://www.mindsetworks.com/page/create-growth-mindset-culture-and-increase-student-achievement.aspx

Boice, Robert. (2000). Advice for new faculty members: Nihil nimus. Boston: Allyn & Bacon.

Bonaccio, Silvia, and Reeve, Charlie L. 2010. The nature and relative importance of students' perceptions of the sources of test anxiety. *Learning and Individual Differences, 20*(6), 617–25. doi:10.1016/j.lindif.2010.09.007

Bramesfeld, Kosha D., and Gasper, Karen. 2010. Sad-and-social is not smart: The moderating effects of social anticipation on mood and information processing. *Journal of Experimental Social Psychology, 46*(1), 146–51. doi:10.1016/j.jesp.2009.09.005

Bruff, Derek. 2009. *Teaching with classroom response systems: Creating Active Learning Environments*. San Francisco: Jossey-Bass.

Brunyé, Tad T., Mahoney, Caroline R., Giles, Grace E., Rapp, David N., Taylor, Holly A., and Kanarek, Robin B. 2013. Learning to relax: Evaluating four brief interventions for overcoming the negative emotions accompanying math anxiety. *Learning and Individual Differences, 27*, 1–7. doi:10.1016/j.lindif.2013.06.008

Buff, Alex, Reusser, Kurt, Rakoczy, Katrin, and Pauli, Christine. 2011. Activating positive affective experiences in the classroom: "Nice to have" or something more? *Learning and Instruction, 21*(3), 452–66. doi:10.1016/j.learninstruc.2010.07.008

Bush, Mirabai. 2011. Mindfulness in higher education. *Contemporary Buddhism, 12*(1), 183–97. doi:10.1080/14639947.2011.564838

Cahill, Larry, Prins, Bruce, Weber, Michael, and McGaugh, James L. 1994. β-Adrenergic activation and memory for emotional events. *Nature, 371*(6499), 702–4.

Carnes, Mark C. 2011, March 6. Setting students' minds on fire. *Chronicle of Higher Education*. Retrieved from http://chronicle.com/article/Setting-Students-Minds-on/126592/

Carnes, Mark C. 2014. *Minds on fire.* Cambridge, MA: Harvard University Press.

Carstensen, Laura L. 1992. Social and emotional patterns in adulthood: Support for socioemotional selectivity theory. *Psychology and Aging, 7*(3), 331–38.

Case, Kim A. 2013. *Deconstructing privilege: Teaching and learning as allies in the classroom.* New York: Routledge.

Cayanus, Jacob L., and Martin, Matthew M. 2008. Teacher self-disclosure: Amount, relevance, and negativity. *Communication Quarterly, 56*(3), 325–41. doi:10.1080/01463370802241492

Chabris, Christopher, and Simons, Daniel. 2011. *The invisible gorilla: And other ways our institutions deceive us.* New York: Harmony Books.

Chambliss, Daniel F., and Takacs, Christopher G. 2014. *How college works.* Cambridge, MA: Harvard University Press.

Chory, Rebecca M., Horan, Sean M., Carton, Shannon T., and Houser, Marian L. 2014. Toward a further understanding of students' emotional responses to classroom injustice. *Communication Education, 63*(1), 41–62. doi:10.1080/03634523.2013.837496

Coan, James A. 2014, January 27. *Why we hold hands: Dr. James Coan at TEDxCharlottesville 2013* [Video file]. Retrieved from http://tedxtalks.ted.com/video/Why-We-Hold-Hands-Dr-James-Coan

Coan, James A., Schaefer, Hillary S., and Davidson, Richard J. 2006. Lending a hand: Social regulation of the neural response to threat. *Psychological Science, 17*(12), 1032–39.

Corkin, Danya M., Yu, Shirley L., Wolters, Christopher A., and Wiesner, Margit. 2014. The role of the college classroom climate on academic procrastination. *Learning and Individual Differences, 32,* 294–303. doi:10.1016/j.lindif.2014.04.001

Craig, Scotty D., Graesser, Arthur C., Sullins, Jeremiah, and Gholson, Barry. 2004. Affect and learning: An exploratory look into the role of affect in learning with AutoTutor. *Journal of Educational Media, 29*(3), 241–50. doi:10.1080/1358165042000283101

Damasio, Anthony. 2005. *Descartes' error: Emotion, reason, and the human brain.* New York: Penguin.

Dass, Ram, and Bush, Mirabai. 1991. *Compassion in action: Setting out on the path of service.* New York: Bell Tower.

D'Mello, Sidney, and Graesser, Art. 2012. Dynamics of affective states during complex learning. *Learning and Instruction, 22*(2), 145–57. doi:10.1016/j.learninstruc.2011.10.001

D'Mello, Sidney, Lehman, Blair, Pekrun, Reinhard, and Graesser, Art. 2014. Confusion can be beneficial for learning. *Learning and Instruction, 29*, 153–70. doi:10.1016/j.learninstruc.2012.05.003

Duckworth, Angela Lee, Quinn, Patrick D., and Seligman, Martin E. P. 2009. Positive predictors of teacher effectiveness. *Journal of Positive Psychology, 4*(6), 540–47. doi:10.1080/17439760903157232

Esseily, Rana, Rat-Fischer, Lauriane, Somogyi, Eszter, O'Regan, Kevin John, and Fagard, Jacqueline. 2015. Humour production may enhance observational learning of a new tool-use action in 18-month-old infants. *Cognition and Emotion*, May, 1–9. doi:10.1080/02699931.2015.1036840

Fiedler, Klaus, and Beier, Susanne. 2014. Affect and cognitive processes in educational contexts. In Reinhard Pekrun and Lisa Linnenbrink-Garcia (Eds.), *International handbook of emotions in education* (pp. 36–55). New York: Routledge.

Finn, Amber N., and Ledbetter, Andrew M. 2013. Teacher power mediates the effects of technology policies on teacher credibility. *Communication Education, 62*(1), 26–47. doi:10.1080/03634523.2012.725132

Flook, Lisa, Goldberg, Simon B., Pinger, Laura, Bonus, Katherine, and Davidson, Richard J. 2013. Mindfulness for teachers: A pilot study to assess effects on stress, burnout, and teaching efficacy. *Mind, Brain, and Education, 7*(3), 182–95. doi:10.1111/mbe.12026

Flore, Paulette C., and Wicherts, Jelte M. 2015. Does stereotype threat influence performance of girls in stereotyped domains? A meta-analysis. *Journal of School Psychology 53*(1), 25–44. doi:10.1016/j. jsp.2014.10.002.

Freeman, Lynne, and Greenacre, Luke. 2011. An examination of socially destructive behaviors in group work. *Journal of Marketing Education, 33*(1), 5–17. doi:10.1177/0273475310389150

Geake, John, and Cooper, Paul. 2003. Cognitive neuroscience: Implications for education? *Westminster Studies in Education, 26*(1), 7–20. doi:10.1080/0140672032000070710

Gendolla, Guido H. E., and Brinkmann, Kerstin. 2005. The role of mood states in self-regulation: Effects on action preferences and resource mobilization. *European Psychologist, 10*(3), 187–98. doi:10.1027/1016–9040.10.3.187

Gerhardt, Megan W. 2014. The importance of being . . . social? Instructor credibility and the millennials. *Studies in Higher Education*, December, 1–15. doi:10.1080/03075079.2014.981516

Ginott, Haim. 1972. *Teacher and child: A handbook for parents and teachers.* New York: Macmillan.

Gladwell, Malcolm. 2007. *Blink: The power of thinking without thinking.* New York: Back Bay.

Gollwitzer, Peter M., and Sheeran, Paschal. 2006. Implementation intentions and goal achievement: A meta-analysis of effects and processes. *Advances in Experimental Social Psychology, 38*, 69–119. doi:10.1016/S0065–2601(06)38002–1

Gooblar, David. 2014, December 17. The pedagogical power of opening up. *Chronicle Vitae.* Retrieved from http://chroniclevitae.com/news /838-the-pedagogical-power-of-opening-up

Graham, Sandra, and Taylor, April Z. 2014. An attributional approach to emotional life in the classroom. In Reinhard Pekrun and Lisa Linnenbrink-Garcia (Eds.), *International Handbook of Emotions in Education* (pp. 96–119). New York: Routledge.

Gross, James J. 1998. Antecedent- and response-focused emotion regulation: Divergent consequences for experience, expression, and physiology. *Journal of Personality and Social Psychology, 74*(1), 224–37.

Gross, James J. 2013a. Emotion regulation: Taking stock and moving forward. *Emotion, 13*(3), 359–65. doi:10.1037/a0032135

Gross, James J. 2015. The extended process model of emotion regulation: Elaborations, applications, and future directions. *Psychological Inquiry, 26*(1), 130–37. doi:10.1080/1047840X.2015.989751

Gruber, Matthias J., Gelman, Bernard D., and Ranganath, Charan. 2014. States of curiosity modulate hippocampus-dependent learning via the dopaminergic circuit. *Neuron, 84*(2), 486–96. doi:10.1016/j.neuron.2014.08.060

Gumbrecht, Jamie. 2015, April 28. Texas A&M Galveston professor fails entire class. Retrieved from http://www.cnn.com/2015/04/28/living/texas-am-professor-fails-class-feat/

Guo, Yi, Klein, Barbara, Ro, Young, and Rossin, Donald. 2007. The impact of flow on learning outcomes in a graduate-level information management course. *Journal of Global Business Issues, 1*(2), 31–39.

Hall, Nathan C., Perry, Raymond P., Goetz, Thomas, Ruthig, Joelle C., Stupnisky, Robert H., and Newall, Nancy E. 2007. Attributional retraining and elaborative learning: Improving academic development through writing-based interventions. *Learning and Individual Differences, 17*(3), 280–90. doi:10.1016/j.lindif.2007.04.002

Harlow, Roxanna. 2003. Race doesn't matter, but . . . : The effect of race on professors' experiences and emotion management in the undergraduate college classroom. *Social Psychology Quarterly, 66*(4), 348. doi:10.2307/1519834

Hatfield, Elaine, Carpenter, Megan, and Rapson, Richard L. 2014. Emotional contagion as a precursor to collective emotions. In C. von Scheve & M. Salmela (Eds.), *Collective emotions* (pp. 108–24). Oxford, England: Oxford University Press.

Haynes, Tara L., Perry, Raymond P., Stupnisky, Robert H., and Daniels, Lia M. 2009. A review of attributional retraining treatments: Fostering engagement and persistence in vulnerable college students. In J. C. Smart (Ed.), *Higher education handbook of theory and research* (vol. 24, pp. 227–70). New York: Springer.

Huk, Thomas, and Ludwigs, Stefan. 2009. Combining cognitive and affective support in order to promote learning. *Learning and Instruction, 19*(6), 495–505. doi:10.1016/j.learninstruc.2008.09.001

Hulleman, Chris S., Godes, Olga, Hendricks, Bryan L., and Harackiewicz, Judith M. 2010. Enhancing interest and performance with a utility value intervention. *Journal of Educational Psychology, 102*(4), 880–95. doi:10.1037/a0019506

Immordino-Yang, Mary Helen. 2011. Implications of affective and social neuroscience for educational theory. *Educational Philosophy and Theory, 43*(1), 98–103. doi:10.1111/j.1469–5812.2010.00713.x

Immordino-Yang, Mary Helen, and Christodoulou, Joanna A. 2014. Neuroscientific contributions to understanding and measuring emotions in educational contexts. In Reinhard Pekrun and Lisa Linnenbrink-Garcia (Eds.), *International Handbook of Emotions in Education* (pp. 607–24). New York: Routledge.

Immordino-Yang, Mary Helen, and Damasio, Antonio. 2007. We feel, therefore we learn: The relevance of affective and social neuroscience to education. *Mind, Brain, and Education, 1*(1), 3–10.

Jeffrey, Kate. 2015, June 6. No more jokes in my lectures [Web log post]. Retrieved from http://corticalia.wordpress.com/2015/06/16/no-more-jokes-in-my-lectures/

Kabat-Zinn, Jon. 2003. Mindfulness-based interventions in context: past, present, and future. *Clinical Psychology: Science & Practice 10*(2): 144–56. doi:10.1093/clipsy.bpg016

Kang, Min Jeong, Hsu, Ming, Krajbich, Ian M., Loewenstein, George, McClure, Samuel M., Wang, Joseph Tao-yi, and Camerer, Colin F. 2009. The wick in the candle of learning: Epistemic curiosity activates reward circuitry and enhances memory. *Psychological Science, 20*(8), 963–73. doi:10.1111/j.1467–9280.2009.02402.x

Kashdan, Todd. 2009. *Curious? Discover the missing ingredient to a fulfilling life*. New York: HarperCollins.

Kashdan, Todd B., and Fincham, Frank D. 2004. Facilitating curiosity: A social and self-regulatory perspective for scientifically based interventions. In P. Alex Linley and Stephen Joseph (Eds.), *Positive Psychology in Practice* (pp. 482–503). Hoboken, NJ: Wiley.

doi:10.2307/528220?ref=no-x-route:795812a57747feba4d7a
90d759589163

Kashdan, Todd Barrett, and Yuen, Mantak. 2007. Whether highly curious students thrive academically depends on perceptions about the school learning environment: A study of Hong Kong adolescents. *Motivation and Emotion, 31*(4), 260–70. doi:10.1007/s11031-007-9074-9

Kaufman, Scott Barry. 2013, September 9. Why education needs more radioactive spiders. [Web log post]. Retrieved from http://blogs.scientificamerican.com/beautiful-minds/why-education-needs-more-radioactive-spiders/

Keller, Melanie M., Chang, Mei-Lin, Becker, Eva S., Goetz, Thomas, and Frenzel, Anne C. 2014. Teachers' emotional experiences and exhaustion as predictors of emotional labor in the classroom: An experience sampling study. *Frontiers in Psychology, 5,* 1442. doi:10.3389/fpsyg.2014.01442/abstract

Keller, Melanie M., Goetz, Thomas, Becker, Eva S., Morger, Vinzenz, and Hensley, Lauren. 2014. Feeling and showing: A new conceptualization of dispositional teacher enthusiasm and its relation to students' interest. *Learning and Instruction, 33,* 29–38. doi:10.1016/j.learninstruc.2014.03.001

Kiverstein, Julian, and Miller, Mark. 2015. The embodied brain: Towards a radical embodied cognitive neuroscience. *Frontiers in Human Neuroscience, 9,* 1–11. doi:10.3389/fnhum.2015.00237

Kornell, Nate, Hays, Matthew Jensen, and Bjork, Robert A. 2009. Unsuccessful retrieval attempts enhance subsequent learning. *Journal of Experimental Psychology: Learning, Memory, and Cognition, 35*(4), 989–98. doi:10.1037/a0015729

Kramer, Adam D. I., Guillory, Jamie E., and Hancock, Jeffrey T. 2014. Experimental evidence of massive-scale emotional contagion through social networks. *Proceedings of the National Academy of Sciences of the United States of America, 111*(24), 8788–90. doi:10.1073/pnas.1320040111

Land, Michael. 2013, March 3. On loves passionate and companionate. [Web log post]. Retrieved from http://servingthestory.com/2013/03/03/on-loves-passionate-and-companionate/

Lang, James M. 2010. *On course: A week-by-week guide to your first semester of college teaching.* Cambridge, MA: Harvard University Press.

Lang, James M. 2013. *Cheating lessons.* Cambridge, MA: Harvard University Press.

Lang, James M. 2015, January 19. Waiting for us to notice them. [Web log post]. Retrieved from http://chronicle.com/article/Waiting-for-Us-to-Notice-Them/151255/

Lang, James M. 2015, February 23. The 3 essential functions of your syllabus: Part 1. [Web log post]. Retrieved from http://chronicle.com/article/The-3-Essential-Functions-of/190243/

Lebreton, Maël, Kawa, Shadia, d'Arc, Badouin Forgeot, Daunizeau, Jean, and Pessiglione, Mathias. 2012. Your goal is mine: Unraveling mimetic desires in the human brain. *Journal of Neuroscience: The Official Journal of the Society for Neuroscience, 32*(21), 7146–57. doi:10.1523/JNEUROSCI.4821–11.2012

Lemov, Doug. 2015. *Teach like a champion 2.0: 62 techniques that put students on the path to college.* Hoboken, NJ: Wiley.

Lowenthal, Patrick R. 2008. Online faculty development and storytelling: An unlikely solution to improving teacher quality. *MERLOT Journal of Online Learning and Teaching, 4*(3), 349–56.

Lyon, Harold. 2014. Rogers' man of tomorrow is today's effective teacher. In Carl R. Rogers, Harold C. Lyon, and Reinhard Tausch, *On becoming an effective teacher: Person-centered teaching, psychology, philosophy, and dialogues with Carl R. Rogers and Harold Lyon* (pp. 30–46). Abingdon, England: Routledge.

Lyons, Ian M., and Beilock, Sian L. 2012. When math hurts: Math anxiety predicts pain network activation in anticipation of doing math. *PloS One, 7*(10), e48076–76. doi:10.1371/journal.pone.0048076

Lyons, Richard E. 2004. *Success strategies for adjunct faculty.* Boston: Allyn and Bacon.

Lukianoff, Greg, and Haidt, Jonathan. 2015, September. The coddling of the American mind. [Web log post]. Retrieved from http://theatlantic.com/magazine/archive/2015/09/the-coddling-of-the-american-mind/399356/

Masters, Ken. 2014. Nipping an education myth in the bud: Poh's brain activity during lectures. *Medical Teacher*, 36(8), 732–35. doi:10.3109/0142159X.2014.916785

Mattarella-Micke, Andrew, Mateo, Jill, Kozak, Megan N., Foster, Katherine, and Beilock, Sian L. 2011. Choke or thrive? The relation between salivary cortisol and math performance depends on individual differences in working memory and math-anxiety. *Emotion*, 11(4), 1000–1005. doi:10.1037/a0023224

McEwan, Ian. 2012, December 6. Ian McEwan: By the book [interview]. *New York Times Book Review*. Retrieved from http://www.nytimes .com/2012/12/09/books/review/ian-mcewan-by-the-book.html?_r=0

McGraw, Peter, and Warner, Joel. 2014. *The humor code*. New York: Simon and Schuster.

Mikels, Joseph A., Maglio, Sam J., Reed, Andrew E., and Kaplowitz, Lee J. 2011. Should I go with my gut? Investigating the benefits of emotion-focused decision making. *Emotion*, 11(4), 743–53. doi:10.1037/a0023986

Morisano, Dominique, Hirsh, Jacob B., Peterson, Jordan B., Pihl, Robert O., and Shore, Bruce M. 2010. Setting, elaborating, and reflecting on personal goals improves academic performance. *Journal of Applied Psychology*, 95(2), 255–64. doi:10.1037/a0018478

Morris, Sean M. 2016, March 23. On love, critical pedagogy, and the work we must do. [Web log post]. Retrieved from http://www .seanmichaelmorris.com/blog//on-love-critical-pedagogy-and-the -work-we-must-do#pq=kCWbDf

Mosteller, Frederick. 1989. The muddiest point in the lecture as a feedback device. *On Teaching and Learning: The Journal of the Harvard-Danforth Center*, 3, 10–21.

Mueller, Pam A., and Oppenheimer, Daniel M. 2014. The pen is mightier than the keyboard: Advantages of longhand over laptop note taking. *Psychological Science*, 25(6): 1159–68. doi:10.1177 /0956797614524581

Myers, Scott A., and Brann, Maria. 2009. College students' perceptions of how instructors establish and enhance credibility through self-disclosure. *Qualitative Research Reports in Communication*, 10(1), 9–16. doi:10.1080/17459430902751808

Napoli, Maria. 2004. Mindfulness training for teachers: A pilot program. *Complementary Health Practice Review, 9*(1), 31–42. doi:10.1177/1076167503253435

Naqvi, Nasir, Shiv, Baba, and Bechara, Antoine. 2006. The role of emotion in decision making: A cognitive neuroscience perspective. *Current Directions in Psychological Science, 15*(5), 260–64.

Niece, Brian K., and Hauri, James F. 2013. Determination of mercury in fish: A low-cost implementation of cold-vapor atomic absorbance for the undergraduate environmental chemistry laboratory. *Journal of Chemical Education, 90*(4), 487–89. doi:10.1021/ed300471w

Nussbaum, Martha C. 2003. *Upheavals of thought: The intelligence of emotions.* Cambridge, England: Cambridge University Press.

Oettingen, Gabriele, Kappes, Heather Barry, Guttenberg, Katie B., and Gollwitzer, Peter M. 2015. Self-regulation of time management: Mental contrasting with implementation intentions. *European Journal of Social Psychology, 45*(2), 218–29. doi:10.1002/ejsp.2090

Oettingen, Gabriele, Pak, Hyeon-ju, and Schnetter, Karoline. 2001. Self-regulation of goal-setting: Turning free fantasies about the future into binding goals. *Journal of Personality and Social Psychology, 80*(5), 736–53.

Patall, Erika A., Cooper, Harris, and Wynn, Susan R. 2010. The effectiveness and relative importance of choice in the classroom. *Journal of Educational Psychology, 102*(4), 896–915. doi:10.1037/a0019545

Paunesku, David, Walton, Gregory M., Romero, Carissa, Smith, Eric N., Yeager, David S., and Dweck, Carol S. 2015. Mind-set interventions are a scalable treatment for academic underachievement. *Psychological Science, 26*(6), 784–93. doi:10.1177/0956797615571017

Pekrun, Reinhard, Frenzel, Anne C., Perry, Raymond P., and Goetz, Thomas. 2007. The control-value theory of achievement emotions: An integrative approach to emotions in education. In Paul A. Schutz and Reinhard Pekrun (Eds.), *Emotion and Education* (pp. 13–36). Amsterdam: Academic Press.

Pekrun, Reinhard, Goetz, Thomas, Titz, Wolfram, and Perry, Raymond P. 2002. Academic emotions in students' self-regulated learning and achievement: A program of qualitative and quantitative research. *Educational Psychologist, 37*(2): 91–105. doi:10.1207/S15326985EP3702_4

Pekrun, Reinhard, and Linnenbrink-Garcia, Lisa (Eds.). 2014. *International Handbook of Emotions in Education.* New York: Routledge.

Perry, Raymond P., Stupnisky, Robert H., Hall, Nathan C., Chipperfield, Judith G., and Weiner, Bernard. 2010. Bad starts and better finishes: Attributional retraining and initial performance in competitive achievement settings. *Journal of Social and Clinical Psychology, 29*(6), 668–700. doi:10.1521/jscp.2010.29.6.668

Pittman, Chavella T. 2010. Race and gender oppression in the classroom: The experiences of women faculty of color with white male students. *Teaching Sociology, 38*(3), 183–96. doi:10.1177/0092055X10370120

Poh, Ming-Zher, Swenson, Nicholas C., and Picard, Rosalind W. 2010. A wearable sensor for unobtrusive, long-term assessment of electrodermal activity. *IEEE Transactions on Biomedical Engineering, 57*(5): 1243–52. doi:10.1109/TBME.2009.2038487

Quinlan, Kathleen M. 2016. How emotion matters in four key relationships in teaching and learning in higher education. *College Teaching, 64*(3), 1–11.

Radel, Remi, Sarrazin, Philippe, Legrain, Pascal, and Wild, Cameron T. 2010. Social contagion of motivation between teacher and student: Analyzing underlying processes. *Journal of Educational Psychology, 102*(3), 577–87. doi:10.1037/a0019051

Rockquemore, Kerry, and Laszloffy, Tracey A. 2008. *The black academic's guide to winning tenure—without losing your soul.* Boulder: Lynne Rienner.

Rotgans, Jerome I., and Schmidt, Henk G. 2014. Situational interest and learning: Thirst for knowledge. *Learning and Instruction, 32,* 37–50. doi:10.1016/j.learninstruc.2014.01.002

Ruthig, Joelle C., Perry, Raymond P., Hladkyj, Steven, Hall, Nathan C., Pekrun, Reinhard, and Chipperfield, Judith G. 2008. Perceived control and emotions: Interactive effects on performance in achievement settings. *Social Psychology of Education 11*(2), 161–80. doi:10.1007/s11218-007-9040-0

Schlam, Tanya R., Wilson, Nicole L., Shoda, Yuichi, Mischel, Walter, and Ayduk, Ozlem. 2013. Preschoolers' delay of gratification predicts their body mass 30 years later. *The Journal of Pediatrics 162*, 90–93. doi:10.1016/j.jpeds.2012.06.049

Schoeberlein, Deborah R., and Sheth, Suki 2009. *Mindful teaching and teaching mindfulness: A guide for anyone who teaches anything.* Simon and Schuster. Boston: Wisdom.

Seung, Sebastian. 2013. *Connectome: How the brain's wiring makes us who we are.* Boston: Mariner.

Shoda, Yuichi, Mischel, Walter, and Peake, Philip K. 1990. Predicting adolescent cognitive and self-regulatory competencies from preschool delay of gratification: Identifying diagnostic conditions. *Developmental Psychology 26*(6), 978–86. doi:10.1037/0012-1649.26.6.978

Silvia, Paul J. 2006. *Exploring the Psychology of Interest.* New York: Oxford University Press.

Silvia, Paul J. 2008. Interest—The curious emotion. *Current Directions in Psychological Science, 17*(1), 57–60. doi:10.1111/j.1467-8721.2008.00548.x

Singh, Nirbhay N., Lancioni, Giulio E., Winton, Alan S. W., Karazsia, Bryan T., and Singh, Judy. 2013. Mindfulness training for teachers changes the behavior of their preschool students. *Research in Human Development, 10*(3): 211–33. doi:10.1080/15427609.2013.818484

Speer, Nicole K., Reynolds, Jeremy R., Swallow, Khena M., and Zacks, Jeffrey M. 2009. Reading stories activates neural representations of visual and motor experiences. *Psychological Science, 20*(8): 989–99. doi:10.1111/j.1467-9280.2009.02397.x

Spencer, Steven J., Steele, Claude M., and Quinn, Diane M. 1999. Stereotype threat and women's math performance. *Journal of Experimental Social Psychology, 35*, 4–28.

Strain, Amber Chauncey, and D'Mello, Sidney K. 2014. Affect regulation during learning: The enhancing effect of cognitive reappraisal. *Applied Cognitive Psychology, 29*(1), 1–19.

Talmi, Deborah. 2013. Enhanced emotional memory: Cognitive and neural mechanisms. *Current Directions in Psychological Science, 22*(6), 430–36. doi:10.1177/0963721413498893

Tannenbaum, Melanie. 2015, January 9. Five things being a Zumba instructor has taught me about science communication [Web log post]. Retrieved from http://blogs.scientificamerican.com

/psysociety/five-things-being-a-zumba-instructor-has-taught-me
-about-science-communication/

Taxer, Jamie L., and Frenzel, Anne C. 2015. Facets of teachers' emotional lives: A quantitative investigation of teachers' genuine, faked, and hidden emotions. *Teaching and Teacher Education, 49*, 78–88. doi:10.1016/j.tate.2015.03.003

Tuitt, Frank, Hanna, Michele, Martinez, Lisa M., Salazar, María del Carmen, and Griffin, Rachel. 2009. Teaching in the line of fire: Faculty of color in the academy. *Thought and Action, 25*, 65–74.

van Doorn, Evert A., van Kleef, Gerben A., and van der Pligt, Joop. 2014. How instructors' emotional expressions shape students' learning performance: The roles of anger, happiness, and regulatory focus. *Journal of Experimental Psychology General, 143*(3), 980–84. doi:10.1037/a0035226

VanLehn, Kurt. 1988. Towards a theory of impasse-driven learning. In Heinz Mandl and Alan Lesgold (Eds.), *Learning Issues for Intelligent Tutoring Systems* (pp. 19–41). New York: Springer.

Varma, Sashank, McCandliss, Bruce D., and Schwartz, Daniel L. 2008. Scientific and pragmatic challenges for bridging education and neuroscience. *Educational Researcher, 37*(3), 140–52. doi:10.3102/0013189X08317687

Voerman, Lia, Korthagen, Fred A. J., Meijer, Paulien C., and Simons, Robert Jan. 2014. Feedback revisited: Adding perspectives based on positive psychology. Implications for theory and classroom practice. *Teaching and Teacher Education, 43*, 91–98. doi:10.1016/j.tate.2014.06.005

Volz, Kirsten G., and Hertwig, Ralph. 2016. Emotions and decisions: Beyond conceptual vagueness and the rationality muddle. *Perspectives on Psychological Science, 11*(1), 101–16. doi:10.1177/1745691615619608

Vygotsky, Lev Semenovich. 1980. *Mind in society: The Development of higher psychological processes.* Cambridge: Harvard University Press.

Wanzer, Melissa B., Frymier, Ann B., and Irwin, Jeffrey. 2010. An explanation of the relationship between instructor humor and student learning: Instructional humor processing theory. *Communication Education, 59*(1), 1–18. doi:10.1080/03634520903367238

Watts, Julie. 2013. Why hyperbonding occurs in the learning community classroom and what to do about it. *Learning Communities Research and Practice, 1*(3), 1–16.

Webb, Thomas L., Christian, Julie, and Armitage, Christopher J. 2007. Helping students turn up for class: Does personality moderate the effectiveness of an implementation intention intervention? *Learning and Individual Differences, 17*(4): 316–27. doi:10.1016/j.lindif.2007.03.001

Willingham, Daniel T. 2004. Ask the cognitive scientist: The privileged status of a story. *American Educator, 28*, 43–45.

Woodall, Denise. 2013. Challenging whiteness in higher education classrooms: Context, content, and classroom dynamics. *Journal of Public and Professional Sociology, 5*(2), 1–17.

Wroe, Nicholas. 2002. Prologue. In Douglas Adams, *The salmon of doubt: Hitchhiking the galaxy one last time* (pp. xv–xxix). New York: Harmony.

Yeager, David S., Henderson, Marlone D., Paunesku, David, Walton, Gregory M., D'Mello, Sidney, Spitzer, Brian J., and Duckworth, Angela Lee. 2014. Boring but important: A self-transcendent purpose for learning fosters academic self-regulation. *Journal of Personality and Social Psychology, 107*(4), 559–80.

Zhang, Qin, and Sapp, David A. 2013. Psychological reactance and resistance intention in the classroom: Effects of perceived request politeness and legitimacy, relationship distance, and teacher credibility. *Communication Education, 62*(1), 1–25. doi:10.1080/0363 4523.2012.727008

INDEX